GET READY FOR 4TH GRADE

Cover design by Josue Castilleja
Cover art by Bernard Adnet

ISBN 0-439-60628-4
Copyright © 2004 by Scholastic Inc. All rights reserved. Printed in the U.S.A.

8 9 10   40   09

New York • Toronto • London • Auckland • Sydney
Mexico City • New Delhi • Hong Kong • Buenos Aires

Teaching *Resources*

Table of Contents

Dear Parent:

Congratulations! You hold in your hands an exceptional educational tool that will give your child a head start into the coming school year.

Inside this book, you'll find one hundred practice pages that will help your child review and learn math, reading, writing, grammar, vocabulary, and so much more! The workbook is divided into 10 weeks, with two practice pages for each day of the week, Monday to Friday. However, feel free to use the pages in any order that your child would like. Here are other features you'll find inside:

- A weekly **incentive chart** to motivate and reward your child for his or her efforts.

- A sheet of **colorful stickers** to add to the incentive chart. There are small stickers for completing the activities each day, as well as a large sticker to use as a weekly reward.

- Suggestions for fun, creative **learning activities** you can do with your child each week.

- A **recommended reading list** of age-appropriate books that you and your child can read throughout the summer.

- A **super-fun, full-color game board** that folds out from the back of the book. You'll also find a sheet of game cards and playing pieces.

- A **certificate of completion** to celebrate your child's accomplishments.

We hope you and your child will have a lot of fun as you work together to complete this workbook.

Enjoy!
The editors

Terrific Tips for Using This Book

1 Pick a good time for your child to work on the activities. You may want to do it around mid-morning, or early afternoon when your child is not too tired.

2 Make sure your child has all the supplies he or she needs, such as pencils and markers. Set aside a special place for your child to work.

3 At the beginning of each week, discuss with your child how many minutes a day he or she would like to read. Write the goal at the top of the incentive chart for the week. (We recommend that a child entering fourth grade read 20 to 25 minutes a day.)

4 Reward your child's efforts with the small stickers at the end of each day. As an added bonus, let your child affix a large sticker at the bottom of the incentive chart for completing the activities each week.

5 Encourage your child to complete the worksheet, but don't force the issue. While you may want to ensure that your child succeeds, it's also important that your child maintain a positive and relaxed attitude toward school and learning.

6 For more summertime fun, invite your child to play the colorful, skills-based game board at the back of the book. Your child can play the game with you or with friends and siblings.

7 When your child has finished the workbook, present him or her with the certificate of completion at the back of the book. Feel free to frame or laminate the certificate and display it on the wall for everyone to see. Your child will be so proud!

Helping Your Child Get Ready: Week 1

These are the skills your child will be working on this week.

Math
- addition/subtraction facts
- adding 3-digit numbers without regrouping

Reading
- making predictions

Writing
- combining sentences
- writing a newsletter

Vocabulary
- antonyms and synonyms

Grammar
- *your* and *you're*

Handwriting
- uppercase cursive letters

Here are some activities you and your child might enjoy.

Listen and Draw Describe an object, animal, or person to your child and ask him or her to draw it. How close does the drawing come to looking like the real thing? Then, ask him or her to describe something for you to draw.

Comic Order Build up your child's sequencing skills. Cut a comic strip into sections. Ask your child to put the strip in the correct order and to explain his or her thinking.

Make a Time Capsule Make a time capsule with your child. Ask him or her to think about what objects could be included in the capsule that will tell people in the future what your family and the time you are living in is like. Put all the items in a container and bury it. (A metal container will work best.)

My Summer Plan Suggest that your child come up with a plan to achieve a goal by the end of the summer. Help him or her map out a way to be successful. Periodically, check to see how he or she is progressing.

Your child might enjoy reading the following books.

Leonardo da Vinci
by Diane Stanley

The Mud Flat Mystery
by James Stevenson

Charlotte's Web
by E.B. White

Goals:

1. Read 5 Books
2. Go to the library
3. Learn to dive
4. Build a treehouse
5. Learn a magic trick

Special Note: The activity for Day 3 of this week is a mini-book. Have your child tear out the page along the perforation and cut along the dotted line. After he or she positions the two sections so the mini-book pages are in sequence, have him or her staple and fold to form a book. Then he or she can complete all the puzzles in the mini-book.

_____'s Incentive Chart: Week 1

Name Here

This week, I plan to read _____ minutes each day.

CHART YOUR PROGRESS HERE.

Week 1	Day 1	Day 2	Day 3	Day 4	Day 5
I read for...	minutes	minutes	minutes	minutes	minutes
Put a sticker to show you completed each day's work.					

Congratulations!

Wow! You did a great job this week!

#1

Place sticker here.

Parent or Caregiver's Signature _____

Great States

Add or subtract. Connect the matching answers to find each state's shape.

Delaware	**16 – 9 =**
Massachusetts	**7 + 7 =**
New Hampshire	**15 – 6 =**
New York	**17 + 1 =**
South Carolina	**14 – 3 =**
Maryland	**15 – 2 =**
Pennsylvania	**14 – 9 =**
Connecticut	**12 + 5 =**
Rhode Island	**7 + 3 =**
North Carolina	**13 – 7 =**
Georgia	**7 + 5 =**
New Jersey	**14 – 6 =**
Virginia	**7 + 8 =**

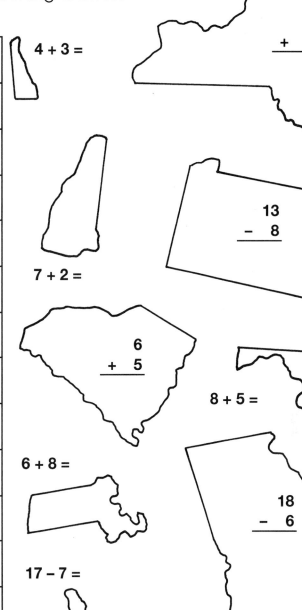

4 + 3 =

$$\begin{array}{r} 9 \\ +\ 9 \\ \hline \end{array}$$

7 + 2 =

$$\begin{array}{r} 13 \\ -\ 8 \\ \hline \end{array}$$

$$\begin{array}{r} 6 \\ +\ 5 \\ \hline \end{array}$$

8 + 5 =

6 + 8 =

$$\begin{array}{r} 18 \\ -\ 6 \\ \hline \end{array}$$

17 – 7 =

18 – 1 =

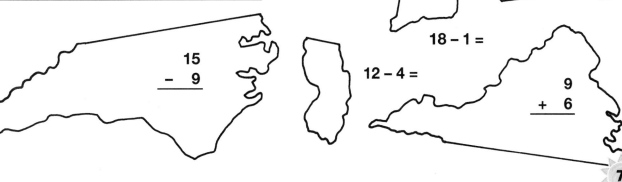

$$\begin{array}{r} 15 \\ -\ 9 \\ \hline \end{array}$$

12 – 4 =

$$\begin{array}{r} 9 \\ +\ 6 \\ \hline \end{array}$$

Grammar Cop

and the Education of Snow White

Snow White has left the seven dwarfs' cottage. She wants to explain her disappearance, but she doesn't really understand the difference between *your* and *you're*. Can you help Grammar Cop fill in the blanks?

Directions: The word *your* or *you're* belongs in each of the boxes. Choose the correct word and write it in.

Dear Dwarfs,

[   ] probably wondering why I left. I have to admit I have gotten tired of [   ] strange habits. It seems like if [   ] not sneezing, then [   ] sleeping or [   ] acting grumpy.

Also, it turned out that the prince wasn't for me. As I said to him, "[   ] really nice, but I don't want to sit around [   ] castle all day while [   ] off slaying dragons."

The other day, I took a good look in the mirror. Sure it said, "[   ] the fairest of them all." But it also said, "Plan for [   ] future. What about [   ] education? [   ] career?"

That was it. "Snow," I said, "say good-bye to [   ] dwarfs. [   ] going back to school."

I hope I haven't hurt [   ] feelings. I appreciate [   ] kindness. [   ] all very generous. But for now, [   ] on [   ] own.

[   ] friend,

Snow White

Remember these basic laws of *your* and *you're*:

• **Your**

Your is the possessive form of *you*. Use it when you are talking about something that belongs to the person with whom you are speaking. (Example: I really like **your** new jeans. Where did you get them?)

• **You're**

You're is a contraction of "you are." Here's a tip: Whenever you write *you're*, read over the sentence and substitute *you are* for *you're*. If the sentence makes sense, you've made the right choice. (Example: I always tell people that **you're** my best friend.)

Scholastic Teaching Resources   *Get Ready for 4th Grade*

Homer's Big Adventure

 Use details from a story to help determine what will happen next. This is called **making predictions**.

Brian was in such a hurry to get to the school bus on time that he forgot to close the door on Homer's cage after he fed him. Homer T. Hamster knew this was his big chance. He crawled out of his cage and ran downstairs, careful to sneak past Brian's mother without being seen. He ducked through a hole in the screen door and stepped out into the great backyard.

"Yippeeee!" cried Homer, throwing his little arms into the air. "I'm free at last!" He zipped through the gate and down the alley. The first thing Homer saw was a huge, snarling German shepherd who thought it was fun to chase anything that could run. "R-r-ruff! R-r-ruff!" Homer scurried here and there only inches ahead of the dog. He barely escaped by hiding under a flowerpot. "Whew, that was close!" he thought. He waited there a while, shaking like a leaf.

Then he crept out into the alley again. He looked this way and that. The coast was clear, so he skipped happily along. He looked up just in time to see the big black tires of a pickup truck that was backing out of a driveway. He almost got squooshed! So, he darted quickly into someone's backyard where a boy was mowing the lawn. R-r-r-r-r-r! Homer had to jump out of the way again.

Back in the alley, he decided to rest somewhere that was safe. He crawled into a garbage dumpster and fell asleep. Later, he heard the sound of a big truck. He felt himself going high up into the air. The dumpster turned upside down, and the lid opened. Homer was falling. "Yikes!" screamed Homer. He had to think fast. He reached out and grabbed the side of the truck, holding on for dear life.

The truck rolled down the alley and into the street. As it turned the corner, Homer was flung off the truck and onto the hood of a school bus. He grabbed onto the windshield wipers as the bus drove to the corner and stopped.

The bus driver exclaimed, "Look, kids! There is a hamster riding on our bus!" All the kids rushed forward to see the funny sight. Homer looked through the windshield at all the surprised faces.

All of a sudden, Homer saw Brian! Brian ran out of the bus and carefully picked up Homer. "Hey, buddy, how did you get out here? Are you okay?" Brian asked as he petted Homer's fur.

1. **What do you think happened next? Color the picture that seems to be the most likely ending to the story.**

2. **Underline the sentence that tells the main idea of the story.**

   Homer hid under a flowerpot to escape from a German shepherd.

   Homer had many exciting adventures after crawling out of his cage.

   Brian was surprised to see Homer riding the school bus.

3. **Do you think Homer will leave his cage again? Write a sentence to tell why or why not.**_____

_____

On another piece of paper, write a paragraph telling about one more adventure Homer might have had while he was out of his cage. Read your paragraph to a friend.

Scholastic Teaching Resources   *Get Ready for 4th Grade*

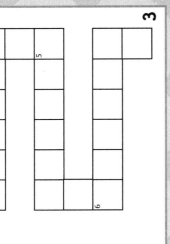

Complete the antonym for each word below. The last letter of each antonym is the first letter of the next antonym. So, in this chain, the first antonym ends with "l" in square 2.

1. horizontal
2. quiet
3. safe
4. sweet
5. forget
6. give

Zigs & Zags

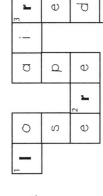

The antonyms in these puzzle chains zig and zag, but the chains hang together. That's because the last letter of each antonym in the chain is also the first letter of the next antonym in the chain.

1. winner
2. break
3. increase
4. shrink
5. wet

Complete the antonym for each word below. The last letter of each antonym is the first letter of the next antonym. So, in this chain, the first antonym ends with "p" in square 2.

1. awake
2. rude
3. tiny
4. save
5. shallow
6. wealthy
7. cooked
8. strongest

6

Complete the antonym for each word below. The last letter of each antonym is the first letter of the next antonym. So, in this chain, the first antonym ends with "w" in square 2.

1. forbid
2. shout
3. conceal
4. most
5. alone
6. fake
7. follower

8

Complete the antonym for each word below. The last letter of each antonym is the first letter of the next antonym. So, in this chain, the first antonym ends with "d" in square 2.

1. backward
2. attack
3. same
4. catch
5. best
6. bottom
7. ashamed

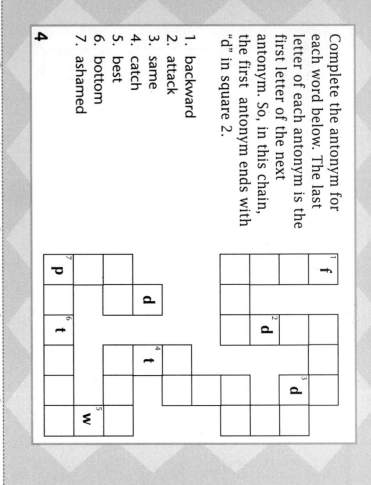

4

Complete the antonym for each word below. The last letter of each antonym is the first letter of the next antonym. So, in this chain, the first antonym ends with "h" in square 2.

1. wise
2. sick
3. old
4. selfish
5. float
6. cruel
7. arrive

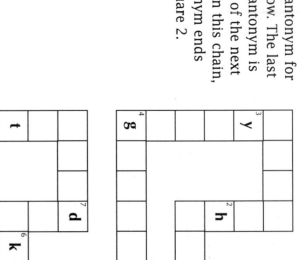

5

Complete the antonym for each word below. The last letter of each antonym is the first letter of the next antonym. So, in this chain, the first antonym ends with "n" in square 2.

1. answer
2. always
3. smooth
4. soft
5. shiny
6. truth
7. cheap
8. full

2

Complete the antonym for each word below. The last letter of each antonym is the first letter of the next antonym. So, in this chain, the first antonym ends with "t" in square 2.

1. guilty
2. wild
3. exit
4. odd
5. wide
6. east
7. thick
8. all

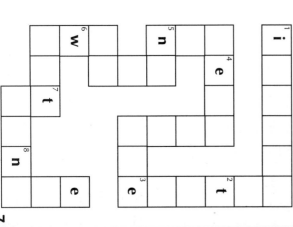

7

It All Adds Up!

Add. Fill in the missing numbers.

3 2 4 + 6 3 ☐ ☐ ☐ 6	2 4 ☐ + ☐ 5 1 7 ☐ 2	☐ 5 5 + 3 ☐ 1 4 8 ☐	2 ☐ 3 + ☐ 1 3 5 2 ☐
4 1 ☐ + 3 ☐ 2 ☐ 3 7	☐ 4 3 + 1 4 ☐ 2 ☐ 9	2 ☐ ☐ + 2 1 6 ☐ 1 8	☐ 3 1 + 4 ☐ ☐ 8 5 3
1 ☐ 2 + ☐ 3 3 3 7 ☐	☐ 4 1 + 1 3 ☐ 6 ☐ 5	3 3 ☐ + ☐ ☐ 3 6 6 8	☐ 1 2 + 2 ☐ 2 9 4 ☐
2 2 ☐ + 3 1 4 ☐ ☐ 4	5 ☐ 4 + ☐ 3 4 8 4 ☐	2 2 4 + 1 ☐ 3 ☐ 6 ☐	☐ 1 6 + 1 3 ☐ 5 ☐ 8

 Joe and Ellie were going to the movies. Joe brought $5.☐0, and Ellie brought $☐.35. If they had $9.75 altogether, how much money did they each have? Show your work.

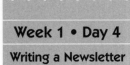

My Family News

Draw a picture about something that happened at home and glue it in this space. Write a sentence about it underneath.

Just for Laughs

This Week's Newsmaker

Scholastic Teaching Resources   *Get Ready for 4th Grade*

Applause for the Clause

Sometimes you can use words such as when, because, while, *and* before *to combine two sentences with related ideas into one sentence with a main clause and a dependent clause. A* **clause** *is a group of words with a subject and a predicate. A* **dependent clause** *cannot stand alone. An* **independent clause** *can stand alone.*

Lee woke up late today. He realized he hadn't set the alarm last night.
When Lee woke up late today, <u>he realized he hadn't set his alarm last night</u>**.**

↑   ↑

This is a dependent clause.   *This is a independent clause.*

When the dependent clause comes before the main clause as in the above sentence, add a comma after the dependent clause. If the dependent clause follows the main clause, you do not need a comma. Here's an example.

Lee was upset. He was going to be late for school.
Lee was upset because **he was going to be late for school.**

Use the word inside the parentheses to combine each pair of sentences into one.

1. **I waited for my parents to get home. I watched a movie. (while)**

   _____

2. **My brother was in his room. He had homework to do. (because)**

   _____

3. **The movie was over. The power went out. (before)**

   _____

4. **This happens all the time. I wasn't concerned. (since)**

   _____

5. **I didn't mind the dark at first. I heard a scratching sound. (until)**

   _____

6. **I found my flashlight. I started to look around. (when)**

   _____

7. **I was checking the living room. I caught Alex trying to hide. (when)**

   _____

a-z

A B C D E F
G H I J K L M
N O P Q R S T
U V W X Y Z

Write.

_____

_____

_____

_____

_____

_____

_____

Scholastic Teaching Resources   *Get Ready for 4th Grade*

Helping Your Child Get Ready: Week 2

These are the skills your child will be working on this week.

Math
- addition of 4-digit numbers without regrouping
- subtraction of 2-digit numbers without regrouping
- identifying multiplication patterns

Reading
- following directions
- identifying fact and opinion
- comparing and contrasting

Writing
- compound sentences

Vocabulary
- suffixes
- analogies

Here are some activities you and your child might enjoy.

Newspaper Treasure Hunt In this special hunt, your child looks for various "treasures" in a newspaper article. The treasures are letters or symbols to which you've assigned a value. For example, a z might be worth $10 and an exclamation point might be $5. Have your child search an article to find out how valuable its "treasure" is.

Two-Minute Lists Give your child two minutes to list as many words as he or she can think of that include double letters.

What's in a Name? Have your child research his or her name. Have him or her find out what the name means. Then tell your child the story of how you chose it. Encourage him or her to find out the meanings of other family members' names as well.

Leaf Survey What kinds of leaves are there in your neighborhood? Have your child do a leaf survey. He or she can collect leaves, use reference books to identify them, and then make a list of all the different trees found in your area.

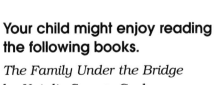

Your child might enjoy reading the following books.

The Family Under the Bridge
by Natalie Savage Carlson

Fourth Grade Rats
by Jerry Spinelli

Hey Kid, Want to Buy a Bridge?
by Jon Scieszka

_____'s Incentive Chart: Week 2

Name Here

This week, I plan to read _____ minutes each day.

CHART YOUR PROGRESS HERE.

Week 2	Day 1	Day 2	Day 3	Day 4	Day 5
I read for...	minutes	minutes	minutes	minutes	minutes
Put a sticker to show you completed each day's work.					

Congratulations!

Wow! You did a great job this week!

#1

Place sticker here.

Parent or Caregiver's Signature _____

Who Said What?

Many words end with a suffix that means "one who" or "one who does an action."

astronom**er**	merch**ant**	superintend**ent**	invent**or**	dent**ist**
librar**ian**	pharmac**ist**	photograph**er**	edit**or**	wait**er**

Read the sentences. Write the word from the box that identifies who said what.

1. **"Your prescription is ready," said the** _____.

2. **"Would you like fries, mashed, or baked potatoes?" asked the** _____.

3. **"I am canceling classes today," the school** _____ **decided.**

4. **"These watches were imported from Germany," explained the** _____.

5. **"Star system Alpha Centauri is 4.3 light-years away," explained the** _____.

6. **"The fine for the overdue books is five dollars," stated the** _____.

7. **"Face the camera and smile," instructed the** _____.

8. **"This incredible engine will revolutionize transportation," explained the** _____.

9. **"It took two years to prepare this book for publication," said the** _____.

10. **"You have a small cavity in this back molar," said the** _____.

What do you want to be when you are an adult? What about your friends? Take a survey to find out. On another sheet of paper, list all the careers suggested.

A New Challenge

When you write, you may want to show how the ideas in two simple sentences are related. You can combine the two sentences by using a comma and the conjunctions and, but, *or* or *to show the connection. And* shows a link between the ideas, but *shows a contrast, and* or *shows a choice. The new sentence is called a* **compound sentence**.

My sister wants to join a football team. My parents aren't so happy about it.
My sister wants to join a football team, but **my parents aren't so happy about it.**

Annie is determined. Her friends think she'd make a great place kicker.
Annie is determined, and **her friends think she'd make a great place kicker.**

Should Annie play football? Should she try something else?
Should Annie play football, or **should she try something else?**

Combine each pair of sentences. Use *and, but,* or *or* to show the connection between the ideas and make a compound sentence.

1. **My sister Annie has always participated in sports. Many say she's a natural athlete.**

   _____

   _____

2. **Soccer, basketball, and softball are fun. She wanted a new challenge.**

   _____

   _____

3. **My sister talked to my brother and me. We were honest with her.**

   _____

   _____

4. **I told Annie to go for it. My brother told her to stick with soccer or basketball.**

   _____

   _____

5. **Will Dad convince her to try skiing? Will he suggest ice skating?**

   _____

   _____

Continue the story about Annie's choice on another piece of paper. Include some compound sentences to tell what happens. Make sure your sentences begin and end correctly. Remember to check for spelling errors.

Scholastic Teaching Resources   *Get Ready for 4th Grade*

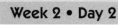
Picking Pairs

For each number, a line connects two things that go together. Find two other things that go together in the same way. Draw a line to connect them.

1. imaginary   number

   ban   make-believe

   allow   forbid

5. core   see

   time   hear

   here   corps

2. secret   midnight

   huge   tiny

   solid   liquid

6. snake   mammal

   tiger   jungle

   skin   reptile

3. clap   permit

   prevent   applaud

   allow   pretend

7. perfect   flawless

   puppy   stare

   stroll   walk

4. terrier   retriever

   lime   strawberry

   penguin   crowd

8. chair   candle

   wick   soft

   cord   lamp

 Tell a partner how the pairs you matched go together.

Majestic Mountains

Add. Use the code to name four different mountain ranges.

N	6,348
R	8,789
A	5,063
I	7,695
O	2,429
K	5,642
E	7,483
C	3,012
Y	2,351
Z	5,234
L	3,721
U	6,704
P	3,827
S	8,749
D	4,907

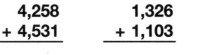

2,033 + 3,030	2,411 + 1,310	2,504 + 1,323	4,328 + 4,421	
◯	◯	◯	◯	

4,258 + 4,531	1,326 + 1,103	1,012 + 2,000	2,321 + 3,321	1,231 + 1,120
◯	◯	◯	◯	◯

1,204 + 1,225	2,113 + 3,121	2,042 + 3,021	3,746 + 5,043	4,131 + 1,511
◯	◯	◯	◯	◯

4,053 + 1,010	2,216 + 4,132	2,506 + 2,401	6,471 + 1,012	7,326 + 1,423
◯	◯	◯	◯	◯

Scholastic Teaching Resources   Get Ready for 4th Grade

Fun With Words

Follow the directions to play each word game.

1. A palindrome is a word that is spelled the same forward or backward. Write each word backward. Circle each word that is a palindrome. Put an X on each word that is not.

   wow _____

   dad _____

   mom _____

   funny _____

   noon _____

   tall _____

   deed _____

2. Some words imitate the noise that they stand for. For example, when you say "pop," it sounds like a popping sound! That is called onomatopoeia. Unscramble each noise word. Write it correctly.

   seechrc _____

   owp _____

   plurs _____

   mobo _____

   lckic _____

   zzisel _____

   chnucr _____

3. Homophones are words that sound alike when you say them but are spelled differently and have different meanings. For example, *see* and *sea* are homophones. Draw a line to match each pair of homophones.

   knot   flew

   break   soar

   flu   not

   sore   write

   right   road

   rode   brake

4. Add or subtract letters from each word to change it into another word. Write the new word.

   peach – ch + r = _____

   shirt – irt + oe = _____

   sports – p – rts + ccer = _____

   love – ove + ike = _____

   stove – st + n = _____

   chicken – c – ick = _____

   brother – bro + nei = _____

 Some names sound funny when you pronounce them backward. For example, Carol would be pronounced Lorac, and Jason would be pronounced Nosaj! Write your name and each of your family members' names backward. Then pronounce each name. Are any of the names palindromes?

TV Commercials

When you watch TV, you see a lot of commercials advertising different products. The people making the commercial want you to buy their product, so they make it sound as good as possible. Some of the things they say are facts, which can be proven. Other things are just the advertiser's opinion about how good the product is or how it will make you feel. Read each advertisement below. Write an *F* in the box beside each fact and an *O* in the box beside each opinion. The first one is done for you.

Eat at Billy Bob's Burgers.

[O] best burgers in town

[F] made with 100% beef

Drive an XJ-80 Sports Car today.

[ ] You'll never want to drive your old car again.

[ ] available in black, red, and silver

[ ] You'll be the Coolest Kid on Your Block with a Pair of Xtreme In-Line Skates!

[ ] on sale for $79.99

Sky-Diving Adventure Video Game

[ ] joystick sold separately

[ ] You'll have hours and hours of fun!

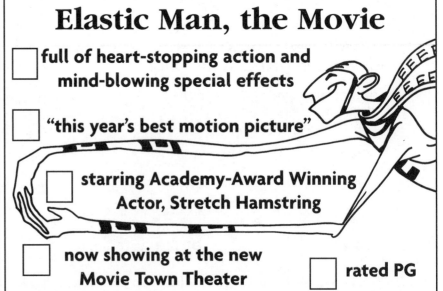

Elastic Man, the Movie

[ ] full of heart-stopping action and mind-blowing special effects

[ ] "this year's best motion picture"

[ ] starring Academy-Award Winning Actor, Stretch Hamstring

[ ] now showing at the new Movie Town Theater

[ ] rated PG

On another piece of paper, design an ad for the Super Squirt Water Gun. Include two facts and two opinions.

Scholastic Teaching Resources   Get Ready for 4th Grade

Sharks

There are over 350 different kinds of sharks. The whale shark is the largest. It is as big as a whale. The pygmy shark is the smallest. It is only about seven inches long.

All sharks live in the ocean, which is salt water, but a few kinds can swim from salt water to fresh water. Bull sharks have been found in the Mississippi River!

Sharks do not have bones. They have skeletons made of cartilage, which is the same thing your ears and nose are made of. A shark's skin is made of spiky, hard scales. The jaws of a shark are the most powerful on earth. When a great white shark bites, it clamps down on its prey and thrashes its head from side to side. It is the deadliest shark.

Sharks eat fish, dolphins, and seals. The tiger shark will eat just about anything. Some fishermen have discovered unopened cans of food, clocks, boat cushions, and even a keg of nails inside tiger sharks. Sometimes sharks even eat other sharks. For example, a tiger shark might eat a bull shark. The bull shark might have eaten a blacktip shark. The blacktip shark might have eaten a dogfish shark. So a tiger shark could be found with three sharks in its stomach!

Some sharks are very strange. The hammerhead shark has a head shaped somewhat like a hammer, with eyes set very far apart. A cookie cutter shark has

a circular set of teeth. When it bites a dolphin or whale, it leaves a perfectly round hole in its victim. The sawshark has a snout with sharp teeth on the outside, which makes it look like a saw. The goblin shark has a sharp-pointed spear coming out of its head, and its ragged teeth make it look scary!

The mako shark is the fastest swimmer. Sometimes makos have been known to leap out of the water, right into a boat! These are just a few of the many kinds of fascinating sharks.

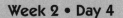

Complete the chart with the name of the correct shark. If the statement is about all sharks, write *all*.

1. the largest shark	whale shark
2. the smallest shark	
3. the deadliest shark	
4. the fastest swimmer	
5. live in the ocean	
6. have skeletons of cartilage	
7. has a sharp-pointed spear coming out of its head	
8. has a head shaped like a hammer	
9. skin of spiky, hard scales	
10. leaves a round bite mark	
11. looks like a saw	
12. has eaten unopened cans, clocks, and boat cushions	

Read more about two different kinds of sharks. On another piece of paper, list two similarities and two differences.

Scholastic Teaching Resources   *Get Ready for 4th Grade*

Find the Patterns

 What is the pattern for the numbers 0, 2, 4, 6, 8, 10, 12, 14, 16, 18?
The pattern shows multiples of 2.

Complete each pattern.

A. **3, 6, 9, 12,** _____, _____, _____, _____, _____

B. **4, 8, 12, 16,** _____, _____, _____, _____, _____

C. **1, 2, 3, 4,** _____, _____, _____, _____, _____

D. **7, 14, 21,** _____, _____, _____, _____, _____

E. **10, 20, 30,** _____, _____, _____, _____, _____

F. _____, **18, 27,** _____, _____, _____, _____

G. **6, 12,** _____, _____, **30,** _____, _____, _____

H. _____, **22,** _____, **44,** _____, _____,**77**

I. **5, 10, 15,** _____, _____, _____, _____, _____

J. **8,** _____, **24,** _____, **40,** _____, _____, _____

K. **10, 12, 14,** _____, _____, _____, **22,** _____, _____

L. _____, **24,** _____, **48, 60,** _____, _____, _____, _____

 **Sam ran every afternoon last week. On Sunday, he ran 3 miles. On Monday, he ran 6 miles.
On Wednesday, he ran 12 miles. How many miles do you think he ran on Tuesday?**

Moving West

Subtract. Follow the even sums to guide the settlers to their new home.

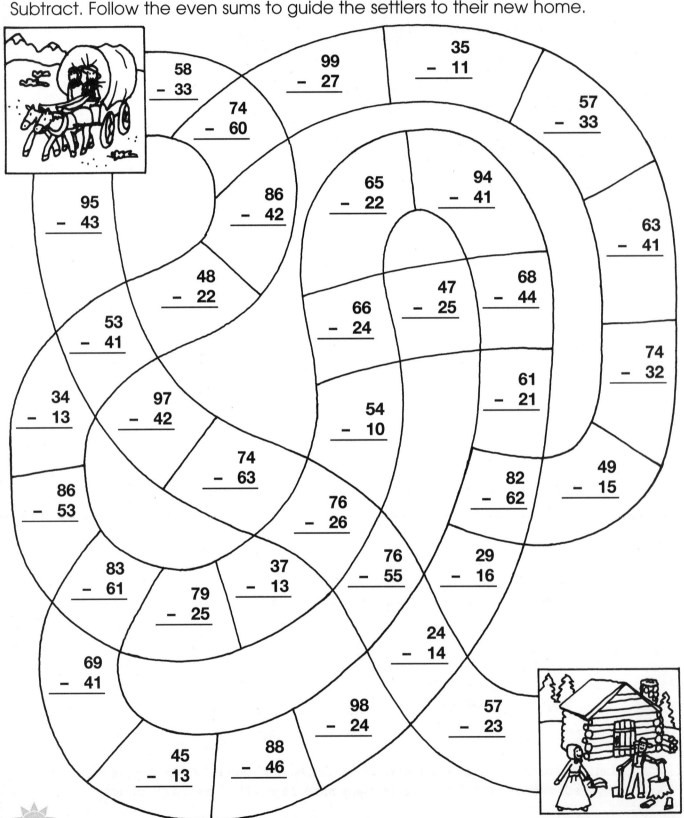

58
− 33

99
− 27

35
− 11

74
− 60

57
− 33

95
− 43

86
− 42

65
− 22

94
− 41

63
− 41

48
− 22

66
− 24

47
− 25

68
− 44

53
− 41

61
− 21

74
− 32

34
− 13

97
− 42

54
− 10

86
− 53

74
− 63

82
− 62

49
− 15

76
− 26

83
− 61

37
− 13

76
− 55

29
− 16

79
− 25

24
− 14

69
− 41

98
− 24

57
− 23

45
− 13

88
− 46

Scholastic Teaching Resources   Get Ready for 4th Grade

Helping Your Child Get Ready: Week 3

These are the skills your child will be working on this week.

Math
- subtraction 2-digit numbers with regrouping
- adding and subtracting money

Reading
- sequencing
- identifying story elements

Writing
- proofreading

Vocabulary
- often-confused words
- roots words

Grammar
- adjectives
- parts of speech

Here are some activities you and your child might enjoy.

Menu Planner Invite your child to plan the family's dinner menu. Be sure he or she heeds the food pyramid nutritional guidelines.

Start Collecting Having a collection is a great way for a child to develop higher-level thinking skills like sorting and analyzing. Encourage your child to start one. Leaves, rocks, stamps, or shells are all easy and fun things to collect.

Invent a Board Game With a few pieces of cardboard and some colored markers, your child can create his or her own board game. To start, suggest he or she model the game on any popular board game. The game might have a special theme, like knights or dinosaurs. Be sure he or she writes out directions for the game. Then play a round!

Flashcard Facts Have your child create his or her own set of multiplication facts flashcards. Then use them on a regular basis to help keep computation skills sharp.

Your child might enjoy reading the following books.

Get the Picture, Jenny Archer?
by Ellen Conford

The Boy Who Loved to Draw: Benjamin West
by Barbara Brenner

Amber Brown Is Not a Crayon
by Paula Danziger

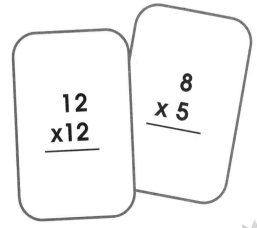

_____'s Incentive Chart: Week 3
Name Here

This week, I plan to read _____ minutes each day.

CHART YOUR PROGRESS HERE.

Week 3	Day 1	Day 2	Day 3	Day 4	Day 5
I read for...	minutes	minutes	minutes	minutes	minutes
Put a sticker to show you completed each day's work.					

Congratulations!

Wow! You did a great job this week!

#1

Place sticker here.

Parent or Caregiver's Signature _____

My Crazy Dream

I don't know why, but I went to school in my underwear. Everyone was laughing! I walked up and down the hall looking for my classroom, but I could never find it. Then I went to the Lost and Found box and put on some clothes. I heard my principal say, "Son, are you lost?" However, when I turned around, it was the President of the United States talking to me. He asked me to fly on his jet with him. As we were flying, I looked out the window and saw a pterodactyl flying next to us! How could that be? They are extinct! It smiled and waved good-bye. Then all of a sudden, the airplane turned into a roller coaster. It climbed upward a million miles, then down we went! For hours and hours we just kept going straight down! The roller coaster finally came to a stop, and I was on an island made entirely of chocolate. I ate a whole tree made of fudge! Then someone sneaked up behind me and captured me. He put me in a pot of boiling water to make soup out of me. I got hotter and hotter and hotter! Finally, I woke up and realized I had fallen asleep with my electric blanket on high.

Number the pictures in the order that they happened in the dream.

 On another piece of paper, draw a picture of a dream you once had. Then write a sentence about the beginning, middle, and end of the dream on separate strips of paper. Have a friend put the sentences in order.

Attack of the Massive Melon!

Don't read this story yet! Give it to a partner and ask him or her to tell you the parts of speech under the blanks below. You give a word for each part of speech, and your partner writes it in the blank. Then he or she writes the words in the story and reads the story aloud.

1. _____
   ADJECTIVE ENDING IN *EST*
2. _____
   NOUN
3. _____
   PLURAL NOUN
4. _____
   ADJECTIVE
5. _____
   NOUN
6. _____
   VERB ENDING IN *ING*
7. _____
   FAMOUS PERSON
8. _____
   ADJECTIVE
9. _____
   ADVERB
10. _____
    NOUN
11. _____
    FAVORITE FOOD
12. _____
    NUMBER
13. _____
    BODY PART
14. _____
    VERB

I decided that I was going to grow the _____ garden in the world. I used a
1
_____ to dig holes in the backyard; then I
2
spread seeds and _____ all around. Pretty
3
soon, my garden started looking _____. I had
4
planted _____ seeds, but a watermelon
5
started _____ out of the ground! It grew
6
and grew. This watermelon became bigger than
_____! Mom said we should eat it before it
7
turned _____. So every day I climbed
8
_____ up a _____, then leaped
9   10
to the top of the melon and cut off huge pieces.
We made watermelon shakes, peanut butter and
watermelon sandwiches, and _____ with
11
watermelon sauce. I've eaten almost nothing but
melon for the last _____ months! Mom
12
said, "Don't look a gift horse in the _____."
13
I sure learned a lesson: Don't bite off more than you
can _____!
14

Scholastic Teaching Resources   Get Ready for 4th Grade

Accept or Except?

 Some words are confusing because they are similar in some way.

Read each sentence and question. Decide which underlined word correctly answers the question. Then write the word.

1. A package just arrived for Jason. Did he <u>accept</u> it or did he <u>except</u> it? _____	2. Sam had a sundae after dinner. Did he have <u>desert</u> or <u>dessert</u>? _____
3. Beth made a right triangle. Does it have three <u>angels</u> or <u>angles</u>? _____	4. All the actors sang and danced the last number. Did they perform the <u>finale</u> or the <u>finally</u>? _____
5. Megan swam the length of the pool underwater. Did she hold her <u>breathe</u> or her <u>breath</u>? _____	6. Aaron's socks slid down to his ankles. Were they <u>loose</u> or <u>lose</u>? _____
7. Jerome just made a dental appointment. Should he mark it on the <u>colander</u> or the <u>calendar</u>? _____	8. Lisa opened the gate and watched as the cows ate grass. Are the cows out to <u>pastor</u> or <u>pasture</u>? _____
9. Meg addressed an envelope. Should she add a <u>coma</u> or <u>comma</u> between the town and state? _____	10. Anna sketched a scene from a story she just read. Did she draw a <u>pitcher</u> or a <u>picture</u>? _____

 Are there any words that confuse you? Record them in a notebook. Include the definition and a sentence using the word. Think of ways to help yourself remember confusing words.

Great Vacations

Subtract. Draw a line from each difference to the vacation spot on the map.

Mount Rushmore	Niagara Falls	Gateway Arch	Four Corners Monument	Statue of Liberty
72 − 27	57 − 29	58 − 39	93 − 19	94 − 29

Grand Canyon	Devil's Tower	Golden Gate Bridge	The Alamo	Old Faithful
82 − 29	93 − 14	64 − 27	66 − 28	94 − 28

 On the map above, mark and write the name of a vacation spot in the United States you would like to visit. Write a subtraction problem for it.

Scholastic Teaching Resources   *Get Ready for 4th Grade*

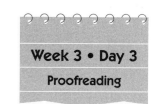

Diary of a Dog

by Louie the Dog

Find and mark the twelve errors. They may be spelling, punctuation, capitalization, or grammar errors.

Dear Diary,

    Today I get up. I did some scrathing because my neck itched. Then I slept. Then I did some sniffing around. Then I slept. Then I barked at the maillman. After that, I took a nap until dinnertime. for dinner, I had pellets in a dish. then I went back to sleep.

Yours truly, **Louie**

Dear Diary,

    Today I saw a small white cats out in the yard. This really made me mad! So I barked a lot. I felt better afterwards. Do you know what I ate for dinner. I ate pellets! I washed it all down with a big slirp of water. Then I go back to sleep.

Yours truly, **Louie**

Dear Diary,

    I just felt like barking todae. So I barked and barked. Then I eaten pellets and went to sleep.

Yours truly, **Louie**

Dear Diary,

    That mailman comes every day! I'm getting tired of barking at him. But I did it anyway? Also, I took a walk. Tomorrow I'll catch up on my sleeping.

Yours truly, **Louie**

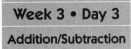

Did You Know?

Add or subtract. Write the letter for the matching number below to find out whose face is on the $50 bill.

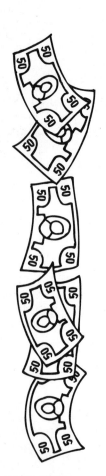

S.	$27.99 + $63.84	L.	$25.59 + $44.96	R.	$71.90 − $59.17
E.	$13.88 + $28.08	S.	$80.31 − $46.16	S.	$25.79 + $38.51
T.	$53.97 − $29.09	Y.	$27.66 + $43.74	N.	$32.48 + $17.77
S.	$94.33 − $56.34	U.	$13.88 + $18.88	G.	$68.74 − $55.29

A. $63.89
   + $26.53

$32.76	$70.55	$71.40	$64.30	$91.83	$41.96	$37.99

$34.15		$13.45	$12.73	$90.42	$50.25	$24.88

Scholastic Teaching Resources   Get Ready for 4th Grade

Best Friends

Amy dreaded recess every day. She did not have any friends to play with. All the girls in her class were paired up with a best friend or in groups, and she always felt left out. So, instead of playing with anyone, Amy just walked around by herself. She wanted to seesaw, but that is something you need to do with a friend. She liked to swing, but she could not go very high. She wished someone would push her to get her started.

One day, the teacher, Mrs. Gibbs, walked up and put her arm around Amy. "What's the matter, Amy? Why don't you play with the other children?" she asked kindly.

Amy replied, "Everyone has a friend except me. I don't have anyone." Mrs. Gibbs smiled and said, "Amy, the way to get a friend is to be a friend." Amy asked, "How do I do that?"

Mrs. Gibbs answered, "Look around the playground. There are three classes of third-graders out here during this recess time. Find someone who is alone and needs a friend. Then go to that person and ask them to play." Amy said she would think about it, but she was afraid she would be too embarrassed. She wasn't sure she could do it.

The next day, Amy noticed a dark-haired girl all alone on the playground. She worked up her courage and walked over to the girl. "Hi! My name is Amy. Do you want to play with me?" she asked.

"Okay," the girl said shyly. As they took turns pushing each other on the swings, Amy found out that the girl's name was Ming. She and her family had just moved from Japan. She did not know anyone and could not speak much English yet. She needed a friend.

"Want to seesaw?" Amy asked. Ming looked puzzled. Amy pointed to the seesaw. Ming smiled and nodded. Amy was so happy. She finally had a friend!

On each blank, write the letter of the picture that correctly answers the question. One answer is used twice.

1. Where does this story take place? _____

2. Who is the main character in the story? _____

   Who are the other two characters in the story? _____ and _____

3. What is the problem in the story? _____

4. How does Amy solve her problem? _____

5. What is Ming's problem? _____

   How does Ming's problem get solved? _____

A. Mrs. Gibbs

B. playground

C. Ming needed a friend, too.

D. Ming

E. Amy

F. Amy asked Ming to play, and they became friends.

G. Amy needed a friend.

Think about what you did during recess or another part of your day. On another piece of paper, list the characters, setting, problem, and solution. Use this list to write a story. Read the story to a friend.

Add an Adjective

An adjective is a word that describes a noun. An adjective often tells what kind or how many.

Look at the noun, *arrow*, at the top of the triangle. Then read each line. The adjectives are underlined. Note how they help to tell more about the arrow.

Complete these triangles. Add adjectives on each line to describe the nouns.

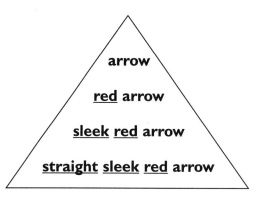

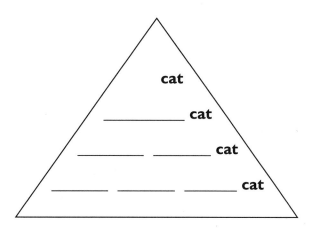

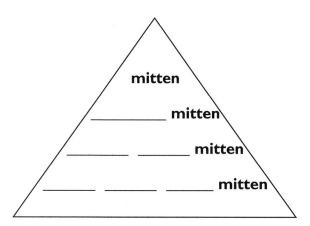

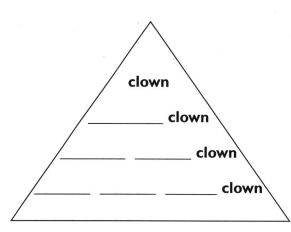

Write a sentence using the noun and all the adjectives from one of the triangles you completed.

_____

_____

The Root of the Matter

A word can have different parts. Many words have a main part, or **root**. *The root contains the basic meaning of the word. For example,* ped *is the root in the word* pedal. *The meaning of* ped *is "foot." Feet are used to push down on the pedals of a bicycle to cause it to move.*

The root is missing from a word in each sentence below. Use context clues and the meaning of the roots in the box to figure out the missing word part. Then write it in the space to complete the word.

pos = place	**phon** = sound	**photo** = light
	port = carry	**pop** = people

1. The _____ulation of our town is just over 20,000.

2. The orchestra will perform a sym_____y by Beethoven next week.

3. The _____ition of the hour hand shows that it is 2:00 P.M.

4. What goods does our country ex_____ to other countries?

5. During _____synthesis, plants use sunlight to make food.

List the words you completed. Then write your own definition for each word. Use a dictionary if you are not sure.

6. _____

7. _____

8. _____

9. _____

10. _____

What other words do you know with the roots *ped, pos, phon, photo, port,* **and** *pop*? **On another sheet of paper, write a word containing each root. Circle the root.**

Scholastic Teaching Resources   *Get Ready for 4th Grade*

Helping Your Child Get Ready: Week 4

These are the skills your child will be working on this week.

Math
- multiplication facts
- identifying fractions
- division

Reading
- making inferences
- using context clues
- identifying overused words

Writing
- combining sentences

Vocabulary
- analogies

Grammar
- quotation marks, commas, and underlining

Here are some activities you and your child might enjoy.

Idiom Illustrations Help your child develop an understanding of idioms by asking him or her to illustrate some. Some examples are "have your cake and eat it too" and "out of the frying pan into the fire."

Compound It Ask your child to see how many compound words he or she can list that contain the word *man*.

ABC Order Read a list of 8–10 words to your child. Then have him or her put the words in alphabetical order.

Weather Watch Have your child track the weather for a week. He or she can record the temperature and precipitation each day on a chart. You might also have him or her compare the weather forecast to the actual weather.

Your child might enjoy reading the following books.

The Piñata Maker
by George Ancona

Rapunzel
by Paul O. Zelinksy

My Name is Georgie: A Portrait
by Jeannette Winter

_____'s Incentive Chart: Week 4

Name Here

This week, I plan to read_____minutes each day.

CHART YOUR PROGRESS HERE.

Week 4	Day 1	Day 2	Day 3	Day 4	Day 5
I read for...	minutes	minutes	minutes	minutes	minutes
Put a sticker to show you completed each day's work.					

Congratulations!

Wow! You did a great job this week!

#1

Place sticker here.

Parent or Caregiver's Signature _____

Multiplication Success

Why are multiplicationists so successful?

To find out, multiply. Then use the code to write the letter of each multiplication sentence on the blank above its product.

A. **10 x 10 =**	G. **3 x 1 =**	N. **12 x 8 =**	S. **6 x 9 =**
B. **6 x 7 =**	H. **9 x 9 =**	O. **6 x 6 =**	T. **6 x 0 =**
C. **5 x 6 =**	I. **8 x 9 =**	P. **11 x 12 =**	U. **5 x 8 =**
E. **7 x 7 =**	L. **12 x 2 =**	Q. **8 x 8 =**	V. **7 x 3 =**
F. **3 x 9 =**	M. **3 x 6 =**	R. **4 x 5 =**	Y. **2 x 8 =**

___ ___ ___ ___ ___ ___ ___ ___ ___ ___ ___ ___
49 21 49 20 16   132 20 36 42 24 49 18

___ ___ ___ ___ ___ ___ ___ ___ ___ ___ ___ ___ ___
0   81 49 16   49 96 30 36 40 96 0   49 20

___ ___ ___ ___ ___ ___
72 96   24 72 27 49

___ ___ ___ ___ ___ ___ ___ ___
42 49 30 36 18 49 54   100

___ ___ ___ ___ ___ ___ ___ ___ ___
30 81 100 24 24 49 96 3   49

___ ___ ___ ___ ___ ___ ___ ___ ___ ___!
0   36   30 36 96 64 40 49 20

Order the Combination

Have you ever noticed how short sentences can make your writing sound choppy? When two sentences have different subjects and the same predicate, you can use the conjunction and *to combine them into one sentence with a compound subject.*

My friends ordered a pepperoni pizza. I ordered a pepperoni pizza.
My friends and I ordered a pepperoni pizza.

When two sentences have the same subject and different predicates, you can use and *to combine them into one sentence with a compound predicate.*

My mom ordered. She had pasta instead.
My mom ordered and had pasta instead.

When two sentences have the same subject and predicate and different objects, you can combine them into one sentence with a compound object using and.

My dad wanted anchovies on his pizza. He also wanted onions.
My dad wanted anchovies and onions on his pizza.

Fill in the missing subject, object, or predicate in each set of shorter sentences. Then combine the sentences by making compound subjects, objects, or predicates using *and*.

1. _____ are sweet and juicy.

   _____ are sweet and juicy.

   _____

2. I _____ about the history of basketball for homework.

   I _____ about the history of basketball for homework.

   _____

3. _____ is so much fun!

   _____ is also so much fun! (Change *is* to *are*.)

   _____

4. I like _____ more than broccoli or cauliflower.

   I like _____ more than broccoli or cauliflower.

   _____

5. I'd like to have _____ for breakfast.

   I'd also like to have _____ for breakfast.

   _____

Scholastic Teaching Resources   Get Ready for 4th Grade

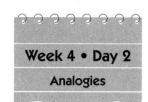

Part of a Whole

Some things are parts of other things. For example, a page is a part of a book. First read each sentence. Note the underlined words. Then tell how the words in the first pair are related and how the words in the second pair are related.

Tip ✔

A <u>page</u> is to a <u>notebook</u> as an <u>eraser</u> is to a <u>pencil</u>.

Say to yourself: A page is part of a notebook, and an eraser is part of a pencil.

1. A <u>map</u> is to an <u>atlas</u> as a <u>definition</u> is to a <u>dictionary</u>. _____

_____

2. A <u>wing</u> is to a <u>bird</u> as a <u>fin</u> is to a <u>fish</u>. _____

_____

3. <u>Sand</u> is to a <u>beach</u> as <u>trees</u> are to a <u>forest</u>. _____

_____

4. A <u>mattress</u> is to a <u>bed</u> as a <u>cushion</u> is to a <u>chair</u>. _____

_____

5. A <u>recipe</u> is to a <u>cookbook</u> as a <u>photo</u> is to an <u>album</u>. _____

_____

Make up a part/whole analogy for a partner to complete.

No Way!

 To divide with remainders, follow these steps.

1. Does 8 x __ = 34? No!

8) 34

2. Use the closest smaller dividend.
8 x 4 = 32

```
    4
8 ) 34
   32
```

3. Subtract to find the remainder.

```
    4
8 ) 34
  - 32
  ____
    2
```

4. The remainder is always less than the divisor.

```
    4 R2
8 ) 34
  - 32
  ____
    2
```

Divide. Then use the code to complete the riddle below.

E. 9) 84	L. 3) 29	S. 7) 67	O. 5) 24
T. 6) 23	N. 6) 47	P. 6) 39	I. 7) 52
O. 4) 19	A. 8) 70	T. 3) 26	S. 9) 55
H. 4) 23	! 7) 45	R. 5) 27	N. 8) 79

Emily: Yesterday I saw a man at the mall with very long arms. Every time he went up the stairs he stepped on them.

Jack: Wow! He stepped on his arms?

Emily:

___ ___ ___ , ___ ___ ___ ___ ___ ___
7 R5 4 R4   4 R3 9 R7   8 R2 5 R3 9 R3

___ ___ ___ ___ ___ ___ ___
9 R4 3 R5 8 R6 7 R3 5 R2 6 R1 6 R3

Monroe's Mighty Youth Tonic

Way back yonder in 1853, a traveling salesman named "Shifty" Sam Monroe rode into our little town of Dry Gulch. I was there that day when Shifty stood on the steps of his **buckboard** selling Monroe's Mighty Youth Tonic. Shifty announced, "Ladies and gentlemen, **lend me your ears**. I, Sam Monroe, have invented a tonic that will give you back your youth. It will **put a spring in your step**. You'll feel years younger if you take a spoonful of this **heavenly elixir** once a day. It contains a **special blend of secret ingredients**. Why, it once made a 94-year-old cowboy feel so young, he went back to **bustin' broncs** again! An old settler that was over 100 felt so young he let out a **war whoop** that could be heard in Pike County! **It's a steal** at only one dollar a bottle. Step right up and get yours now." Well, I wondered what those secret ingredients were, so I bought a bottle and tasted it. It tasted like nothing but sugar water. So I hid behind Shifty Sam's wagon and waited for the crowd to **mosey** on home. When Shifty went inside to make some more tonic, I **kept my eye on him**. Sure enough, he mixed sugar and water and added a drop of vanilla. We'd been **hornswoggled**! I **hightailed it** right then over to the sheriff's office and had him arrest that no-good varmint. Old Shifty is now spending the rest of his "mighty youth" **behind bars**!

Howdy, partner! Read the bolded words in the story on page 47. What do they mean? Hitch up the words on the left with the correct meanings on the right.

1. **way back yonder**

2. **buckboard**

3. **Lend me your ears.**

4. **Put a spring in your step.**

5. **heavenly elixir**

6. **special blend of secret ingredients**

7. **bustin' broncs**

8. **war whoop**

9. **It's a steal!**

10. **mosey**

11. **kept my eye on him**

12. **hornswoggled**

13. **hightailed it**

14. **no-good varmint**

15. **behind bars**

walk slowly

cheated; tricked

watched him closely

making wild horses gentle

ran quickly

evil creature

Listen to me.

in jail

wagon

You are getting it for a low price.

I won't tell what's in it.

makes you feel peppy

many years ago

loud yell

wonderful tonic

Where Am I?

Making **inferences** *means to use information in a story to make judgments about information not given in the story.*

Read each riddle below. Look for clues to help you answer each question.

1. It is dark in here. I hear bats flying. With my flashlight, I see stalactites hanging above me. I hear water dripping. Where am I?

   _____

2. Let's sit in the front row! Ha ha ha! That's funny . . . a cartoon about a drink cup that is singing to a candy bar. That makes me hungry. I think I'll go get some popcorn before it starts. Where am I?

   _____

3. This thing keeps going faster and faster, up and down, and over and around. It tickles my tummy. The girls behind me are screaming. I hope I don't go flying out of my seat! Where am I?

   _____

4. I can see rivers and highways that look like tiny ribbons. I am glad I got to sit by the window. Wow, we are in a cloud! Yes, ma'am. I would like a drink. Thank you. Where am I?

   _____

5. I am all dressed up, sitting here quietly with my parents. The flowers are pretty. The music is starting. Here she comes down the aisle. I wish they would hurry so I can have some cake! Where am I?

   _____

6. Doctor, can you help my dog? His name is Champ. He was bitten by a snake, and his leg is swollen. I hope he will be all right. Where am I?

   _____

7. How will I ever decide? Look at all the different kinds. There are red hots, chocolates, candy corn, gummy worms, jawbreakers, and lollipops. Boy, this is my favorite place in the mall! Where am I?

   _____

8. This row has carrots growing, and this one has onions. The corn is getting tall. The soil feels dry. I better water the plants today. Don't you think so, Mr. Scarecrow? Where am I?

   _____

 On another piece of paper, write two "Where Am I?" riddles of your own. Read your riddles to someone else and have them guess where you are.

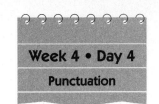
Using Punctuation

Quotation marks show the exact words of a speaker. **Commas** appear between the day and year in a date, between the city and state in a location, between the lines of an address, and after all but the last item in a series. **Underlining** shows book titles.

A. **Read each sentence. Add any missing commas.**

1. Mrs. Wu's bank is located at 92 Maple
   Avenue Inwood Texas 75209.

2. She opened an account there on September 8 2001.

3. She also uses the branch office in Lakewood Texas.

4. That branch is open weekdays Saturdays and some evenings.

5. The main office is closed Saturdays Sundays and all holidays.

6. Mrs. Wu saw Ms. Ames Mr. Pacheco and Mrs. Jefferson at the bank
   on Saturday.

7. They carried checks bills and deposits.

8. Mr. Pacheco has had an account at that bank since May 2 1974.

B. **Read the sentences below. Add any missing quotation marks, commas, or underlining.**

1. My favorite author is Jerry Spinelli   said Rick.

2. Spinelli was born on February 1 1941.

3. His home town is Norristown Pennsylvania.

4. What are your favorite books by him? asked Teresa.

5. I like Maniac Magee Dump Days and Fourth Grade Rats   replied Rick.

Write a sentence that tells your own mailing address. Then name three things you enjoy receiving in the mail, such as letters from friends, magazines, or catalogs.

Scholastic Teaching Resources   *Get Ready for 4th Grade*

Numerous, Spectacular Words

 When you write, do you sometimes overuse descriptive words like good, bad, nice, *or* wonderful? *Overused words can make your writing boring.*

> *The weather was **good** for our first camping trip. (fair)*
> *A ranger gave us some really **good** tips about the park. (useful)*
> *Mom thought the campsite near the stream was **good**. (lovely)*
> *My older brother is a **good** fly fisherman. (skilled)*
> *He said his equipment is too **good** for me to use, though! (valuable)*

Now reread the sentences. This time use the words in parentheses in place of the word good. *You can use a thesaurus to help find words. A thesaurus is a reference book that gives synonyms and antonyms for words.*

Identify eight frequently overused descriptive words in the passage below and list them in the answer spaces. Next, use a thesaurus to write three synonyms for each word, or write three synonyms you know. Then revise the passage. Use editing symbols to cross out the overused words and add the more effective synonyms to replace them.

Our family has a dog named Scooter. He's normally very good until it's time to bathe him. That's when our nice, little terrier turns into a big, furry monster. Scooter isn't really bad. He's just hard to handle when he doesn't want to do something. I think he's afraid of water. You should see how sad he looks once we manage to get him into the tub.

1. _____ _____

2. _____ _____

3. _____ _____

4. _____ _____

5. _____ _____

6. _____ _____

7. _____ _____

8. _____ _____

 Reread a composition you wrote last year. Look for overused words and then use a thesaurus to find other words that you could use instead to make your writing more interesting.

What Is a Fraction?

A fraction consists of two parts.

 $\frac{3}{4}$ The **numerator** tells how many parts are being identified.
The **denominator** tells the total number of equal parts in the whole.

Write the name of each fraction.

A.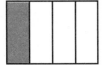

——— ——— ——— ——— ———

B.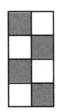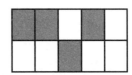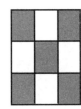

——— ——— ——— ——— ———

C.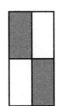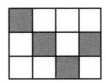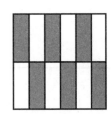

——— ——— ——— ——— ———

Scholastic Teaching Resources   Get Ready for 4th Grade

Helping Your Child Get Ready: Week 5

These are the skills your child will be working on this week.

Math
- multiplication facts
- 2-digit multiplication; logic

Reading
- finding the main idea
- comparing and contrasting

Writing
- using similes and metaphors
- expanding sentences

Vocabulary
- idioms

Grammar
- verb tenses
- contractions

Here are some activities you and your child might enjoy.

Homograph Duos Ask your child to use each of the homonyms *pen*, *uniform*, and *base* in two sentences that each show one of the word's meanings. For example, *Joe's pen was out of ink* and *The pigs ran out of the pen.*

What's Your Estimate Ask your child to estimate how many times in 60 seconds he or she can …
  a) say "Alabama"   **b)** touch his or her toes

Then have him or her try each activity and compare the results with the estimate.

Order, Please! Have your child put these time period words in order from shortest to longest.

hour	week	millisecond
decade	day	minute

Tongue Twisters Have fun with tongue twisters. See how many times your child can say a tongue twister in one minute. Here are some examples to get you started: "Some shun sunshine" and "How much wood would a wood chuck chuck if a wood chuck could chuck wood?"

Some shun sunshine

Your child might enjoy reading the following books.

The Dragons Are Singing Tonight
by Jack Prelutsky

Ben and Me
by Robert Lawson

Accidents May Happen
by Charlotte Foltz Jones

_____'s Incentive Chart: Week 5

Name Here

This week, I plan to read _____ minutes each day.

CHART YOUR PROGRESS HERE.

Week 5	Day 1	Day 2	Day 3	Day 4	Day 5
I read for...	minutes	minutes	minutes	minutes	minutes
Put a sticker to show you completed each day's work.					

Congratulations!

Wow! You did a great job this week!

Place sticker here.

Parent or Caregiver's Signature _____

Colorful Clues

You can compare two things that are not alike in order to give your readers a clearer and more colorful picture. When you use like *or* as *to make a comparison, it is called a* **simile**.

Max is as slow as molasses when he doesn't want to do something.
My sister leaped over the puddles like a frog to avoid getting her shoes wet.
The angry man erupted like a volcano.

When you make a comparison without like *or* as*, it is called a* **metaphor**. *You compare things directly, saying the subject is something else.*

The disturbed anthill was a whirlwind of activity.
The oak trees, silent sentries around the cabin, stood guard.
Jenny and I were all ears as we listened to the latest gossip.

Finish the metaphors and similes.

1. **Crowds of commuters piled into the subway cars like** _____

   _____

2. **Chirping crickets on warm summer night are** _____

   _____

3. **After rolling in the mud, our dog looked like** _____

4. **Happiness is** _____

5. **Just learning to walk, the toddler was as wobbly as** _____

   _____

6. **After scoring the winning point, I felt as** _____

   _____

7. **Having a tooth filled is about as much fun as** _____

   _____

8. **A summer thunderstorm is** _____

   _____

9. _____ **is** _____

10. _____ **is like** _____

Piece of Cake!

Piece of cake *is an example of a common* **idiom**, *or expression. It means "an easy task." It is difficult to understand the meaning of the idiom by using the ordinary meaning of the words.*

What does the idiom in each sentence mean? Circle the letter of the meaning that makes the most sense.

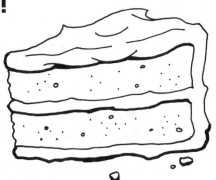

1. Jason was so tired that he *hit the hay* right after dinner.
   a. went to bed   **b.** went back to work   **c.** cut the grass

2. Do not waste your money on this video because it is *for the birds*.
   a. worthless   **b.** fantastic   **c.** expensive

3. Jasmine was *down in the dumps* after losing the game.
   a. smelly   **b.** excited   **c.** sad

4. "Rap music is definitely *not my cup of tea*," said Jack's grandmother.
   a. not cheap   **b.** not to my liking   **c.** not hot enough

5. Ben and Lisa do not *see eye to eye* about which movie to watch.
   a. agree   **b.** disagree   **c.** argue

6. "I don't recall his name," said Kim, "but his face *rings a bell*."
   a. is unfamiliar   **b.** stirs a memory   **c.** appears

7. Carlos has been *on cloud nine* since winning the contest.
   a. very unhappy   **b.** unfriendly   **c.** joyous

8. The two old men were sitting on the park bench *chewing the fat.*
   a. feeding the squirrels   **b.** having a friendly chat   **c.** eating lunch

9. Although he was losing by 20 points, Alex refused to *throw in the towel.*
   a. give up   **b.** take a shower   **c.** do laundry

10. I *kept a straight face* when I saw Ann's wild new hairdo.
    a. poked fun   **b.** kept from laughing   **c.** stared

Listen for idioms in conversations you hear throughout the day. Write them down in a notebook. If you do not know what an idiom means, try to find out.

Scholastic Teaching Resources   Get Ready for 4th Grade

Maze

Trace a path to Ocean Beach through seven correctly spelled contractions. You cannot pass through any areas with misspelled contractions; they act like blocks and force you to go back and try a different route.

What a Nose!

An elephant's trunk is probably the most useful nose in the world. Of course, it is used for breathing and smelling, like most noses are. However, elephants also use their trunks like arms and hands to lift food to their mouths. They suck water into their trunks and pour it into their mouths to get a drink. Sometimes they spray the water on their backs to give themselves a cool shower. An adult elephant can hold up to four gallons of water in its trunk. Elephants can use their trunks to carry heavy things, such as logs that weigh up to 600 pounds! The tip of the trunk has a little knob on it that the elephant uses like a thumb. An elephant can use the "thumb" to pick up something as small as a coin. Trunks are also used for communication. Two elephants that meet each other touch their trunks to each other's mouth, kind of like a kiss. Sometimes a mother elephant will calm her baby by stroking it with her trunk. Can your nose do all those things?

Find the statement below that is the main idea of the story. Write *M.I.* in the elephant next to it. Then find the details of the story. Write *D* in the elephant next to each detail. Be careful! There are two sentences that do not belong in this story.

 Elephants use their trunks to greet each other, like giving a kiss.

 Elephants use their trunks to give themselves a shower.

 Some people like to ride on elephants.

 Elephants can carry heavy things with their trunks.

 Mother elephants calm their babies by stroking them with their trunks.

 Elephants use their trunks to eat and drink.

 Elephants use their noses for smelling and breathing.

 Elephants have very useful noses.

 Giraffes are the tallest animals in the world.

 On another piece of paper, finish this story: *When I was on safari, I looked up and saw a herd of elephants.* **Underline the main idea.**

Stretching Sentences

 A sentence is more interesting when it includes more than just a subject and a verb. It may tell where or when the sentence is happening. It may also tell why something is happening.

Write a sentence describing each set of pictures. Include a part that tells where, why, or how something is happening.

1. _____

2. _____

3. _____

4. _____

 Find a cartoon in the newspaper. Use the pictures to write a sentence on another piece of paper that includes a subject, a verb, and a part that tells where, when, or why.

Geometric Multiplication

Multiply. Color each triangle with an even product orange. Color each triangle with an odd product blue.

8 x 6 = ___	9 x 4 = ___	8 x 9 = ___	8 x 12 = ___
7 x 9 = ___	7 x 7 = ___	9 x 3 = ___	9 x 11 = ___
7 x 7 = ___	4 x 6 = ___	8 x 7 = ___	1 x 7 = ___
8 x 8 = ___	9 x 5 = ___	5 x 7 = ___	8 x 10 = ___
6 x 9 = ___	9 x 9 = ___	7 x 3 = ___	6 x 6 = ___
7 x 11 = ___	5 x 8 = ___	6 x 3 = ___	9 x 7 = ___
1 x 9 = ___	5 x 9 = ___	7 x 5 = ___	3 x 9 = ___
7 x 10 = ___	7 x 6 = ___	9 x 8 = ___	6 x 12 = ___

Maria was decorating a picture frame for her friend's birthday. She chose seven different-sized, diamond-shaped tiles to glue around the frame. There was enough room to glue four colors of each size of tile. How many tiles did she use altogether to decorate the frame? On another piece of paper, solve this problem and draw a picture of what the frame might look like.

60

Special Charts

Comparing and **contrasting** means to show the similarities and differences of things. A Venn diagram is a chart made of overlapping circles that can be used to organize the similarities and differences. The overlapping parts of the circles show how things are similar. The other part of the circles show how things are different.

Joe, Kim, and Rob each got a lunch tray, went through the lunch line, and sat together to eat. These students all had the same lunch menu, but each one only ate what he or she liked. Joe ate chicken nuggets, green beans, applesauce, and carrots. Rob ate chicken nuggets, green beans, a roll, and corn. Kim ate chicken nuggets, a roll, applesauce, and salad.

Today's Menu

chicken nuggets
corn
green beans
carrots
salad
roll
applesauce

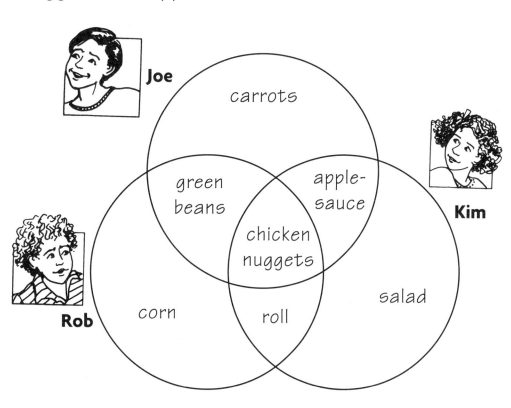

1. What food did all three students eat? _____
2. What did Joe and Rob eat that Kim did not? _____
3. What did Joe and Kim eat that Rob did not? _____
4. What did Kim and Rob eat that Joe did not? _____
5. What did Joe eat that no one else ate? _____
6. What did Rob eat that no one else ate? _____
7. What did Kim eat that no one else ate? _____

Present- and Past-Tense Verbs

Present-tense verbs show action that is happening now. They agree in number with who or what is doing the action. **Past-tense verbs** show action that took place in the past. Most past-tense verbs end in -ed.

A. **Read each sentence. If the underlined verb is in the present tense, write present on the line. If it is in the past tense, write past.**

1. We <u>worked</u> together on a jigsaw puzzle. _____

2. Mom <u>helped</u> us. _____

3. She <u>enjoys</u> puzzles, too. _____

4. Tom <u>picked</u> out the border pieces. _____

5. He <u>dropped</u> a puzzle piece on the floor. _____

6. I <u>looked</u> for the flower pieces. _____

7. Dad <u>likes</u> crossword puzzles better. _____

8. My little sister <u>watches</u> us. _____

9. Mom <u>hurries</u> us before dinner. _____

10. We <u>rushed</u> to finish quickly. _____

B. **Underline the verb in each sentence. Then rewrite the sentence. Change the present-tense verb to the past. Change the past-tense verb to the present.**

1. The man crosses the river.

_____

2. He rowed his boat.

_____

Scholastic Teaching Resources   Get Ready for 4th Grade

In the Wink of an Eye

Solve the problems. If the answer is even, connect the dot beside each problem to the heart on the right- and left-hand sides of the circle. If the answer is odd, do nothing. Two lines have been drawn for you.

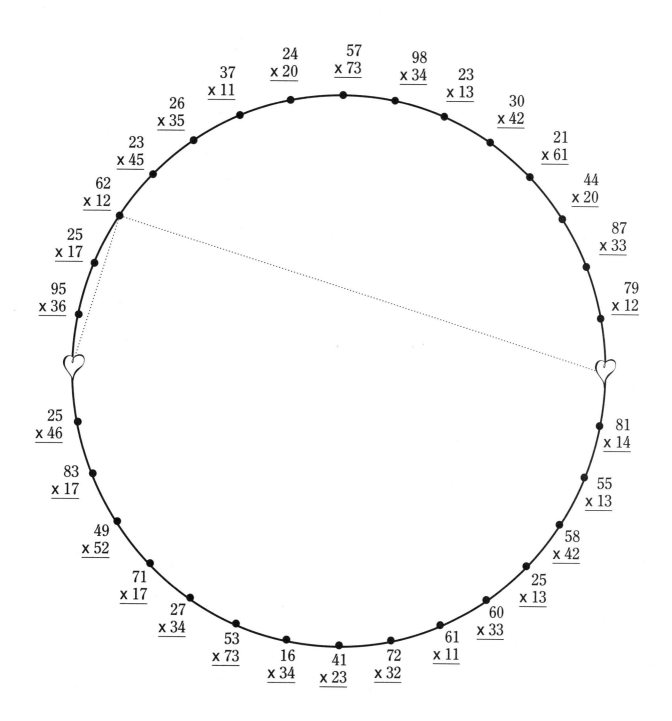

Swimming in Logic

Logic clues put the final finish on our swimming competition. Read the clues and place these swimmers in the correct finishing order.

Dive Into These Clues!

1. Asher finished before Grace but after Emily.
2. Grace finished after Alicia but before Finn and Dillon.
3. Alicia finished before Emily.
4. Finn came in last.

Results:

1st _____

2nd _____

3rd _____

4th _____

5th _____

6th _____

Helping Your Child Get Ready: Week 6

These are the skills your child will be working on this week.

Math
- division with remainders
- money

Reading
- visualizing
- drawing conclusions

Writing
- expanding sentences
- combining sentences

Vocabulary
- antonyms

Grammar
- capitalization
- statements and questions

Here are some activities you and your child might enjoy.

Quick Look Ask your child to look around your kitchen and find ten or more items that begin with the letter S.

Listen Up Help your child develop good listening and memorization skills. Read the names of the first five presidents of the United States (listed here) two times. Then ask your child to repeat the list back to you in order.

George Washington, John Adams, Thomas Jefferson, James Madison, and James Monroe

Birthday Futures Have your child figure out what day of the week his or her birthday will fall on this year, next year, and the year after that. Ask him or her to describe any pattern he or she notices.

Vegetable Know-How The vegetables we eat come from different parts of plants. Ask your child to keep track of the vegetables you eat for dinner for one week. Then have him or her create a chart to show which part of the plant each vegetable comes from.

Your child might enjoy reading the following books.

What Do Authors Do?
by Eileen Christelow

In the Year of the Boar and Jackie Robinson
by Betty Bao Lord

Justin and the Best Biscuits in the World
by Mildred Pitts Walter

_____'s Incentive Chart: Week 6

Name Here

This week, I plan to read _____ minutes each day.

CHART YOUR PROGRESS HERE.

Week 6	Day 1	Day 2	Day 3	Day 4	Day 5
I read for...	minutes	minutes	minutes	minutes	minutes
Put a sticker to show you completed each day's work.					

Congratulations!

Wow! You did a great job this week!

#1

Place sticker here.

Parent or Caregiver's Signature _____

Grammar Cop
and the case of the missing capital letters

The person who wrote this letter didn't really understand the laws of capital letters. Can you help Grammar Cop find the mistakes?

Circle the letters that should have been capitalized.
Hint: There are 19 mistakes.

Dear cinderella and Prince Charming,

there must be a terrible mistake! the stepsisters and I have not yet received an invitation to your wedding. i keep telling the stepsisters that the invitation will arrive soon. i'm getting worried that our invitation got lost. i hear you often have problems with the unicorns that deliver the palace mail.

I'm sure you intend to invite us! After all, you were always my special favorite. How i spoiled you! i let you do all the best chores around the house. are you still mad about that trip to disney world? i don't know how we could have forgotten you! anyway, florida is too hot in the summer.

so cinderella, dear, please send along another invitation as soon as you can. i know how busy you are in your new palace. if you need any cleaning help, i can send one of your stepsisters along. they both miss you so much!

Best wishes,

Your not really so wicked stepmother

Remember these basic laws of capital letters:

• **Names**
Always capitalize someone's proper name. (Example: **G**ina, **K**enneth, **T**yrone)

• **Places**
Always capitalize the name of the town, city, state, and country. (Example: I live in **O**rchard **B**each, **C**alifornia, which is in the **U**nited **S**tates.)

• *I*
Always capitalize the letter *I* when it stands for a person. (Example: **I** am in fourth grade, and **I**'m ten years old.)

• **First letter**
Always capitalize the first letter of the first word of a sentence.

Scholastic Teaching Resources   Get Ready for 4th Grade

Division Decoder

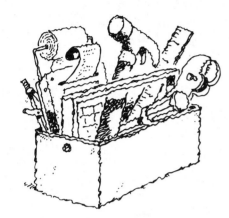

Riddle: What kind of tools do you use for math?

Find each quotient. Then use the Decoder to solve the riddle by filling in the spaces at the bottom of the page.

1. $8 \div 2$ = _____

2. $10 \div 5$ = _____

3. $24 \div 4$ = _____

4. $50 \div 10$ = _____

5. $72 \div 9$ = _____

6. $32 \div 10$ = _____

7. $48 \div 7$ = _____

8. $29 \div 3$ = _____

9. $65 \div 8$ = _____

10. $92 \div 6$ = _____

Decoder

8 I
3 remainder 2 L
7 .... W
8 remainder 1 ..... S
6 .... U
9 .... A
15 remainder 3 ... B
4 L
2 remainder 3 ..... D
9 remainder 2 ..... T
1 .... F
7 remainder 6 ..... N
6 remainder 6 I
2 .... E
11 .... O
15 remainder 2 ... P
2 remainder 5 X
10 C
5 .... R

"M ___ ___ ___ ___" ___ ___ ___ ___ ___ ___
  3 1 8 5 10 6 7 2 4 9

Scholastic Teaching Resources Get Ready for 4th Grade

On the Contrary

Antonyms *are words that have opposite or nearly opposite meanings. A* **suffix** *is added to the end of a word to change its meaning. The suffix* -ous *means "having" or "full of."*

Write a word from the box that is the antonym of the clue word to complete the crossword puzzle.

tiny	silly	unclear	unknown	stingy	tasteless
calm	few	rude	careless	safe	timid

Across

1. delicious
4. anxious
5. numerous
6. courteous
10. enormous
11. cautious

Down

1. courageous
2. dangerous
3. generous
7. famous
8. serious
9. obvious

What other words do you know that end with *-ous*? **On another sheet of paper, make a list of five words. Write your own definition for each word.**

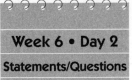

Statements and Questions

A **statement** begins with a capital letter and ends with a period. A **question** begins with a capital letter and ends with a question mark.

A. Rewrite each sentence correctly. Begin each sentence with a capital letter. Use periods and question marks correctly.

1. can we take a taxi downtown

_____

2. where does the bus go

_____

3. the people on the bus waved to us

_____

4. we got on the elevator

_____

5. should I push the elevator button

_____

B. Write a question. Then write an answer that is a statement.

1. Question: _____

_____

2. Statement: _____

_____

Scholastic Teaching Resources   *Get Ready for 4th Grade*

Stretch It!

 A sentence includes a subject and a verb. A sentence is more interesting when it also includes a part that tells where, when, or why.

Add more information to each sentence by telling where, when, or why. Write the complete new sentence.

1. **Mom is taking us shopping.** Where?

   _____

2. **The stores are closing.** When?

   _____

3. **We need to find a gift for Dad.** Why?

   _____

4. **I will buy new jeans.** Where?

   _____

5. **We may eat lunch.** When?

   _____

 Find two sentences in your favorite book that include a subject, verb, and a part that tells where, when, or why. Write the sentences on another piece of paper.

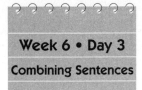

Let's Eat Out!

Two sentences can be combined to make one sentence by using the words **although,** **after, because, until,** *and* **while.**

Choose a word from the menu to combine the two sentences into one sentence.

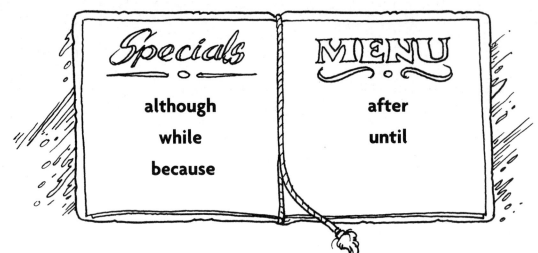

Specials

although

while

because

MENU

after

until

1. We are eating out tonight. Mom worked late.

   _____

2. We are going to Joe's Fish Shack. I do not like fish.

   _____

3. Dad said I can play outside. It's time to leave.

   _____

4. We can play video games. We are waiting for our food.

   _____

5. We may stop by Ida's Ice Cream Shop. We leave the restaurant.

   _____

Read the back of a cereal box. Find two sentences that could be combined.

Scholastic Teaching Resources   *Get Ready for 4th Grade*

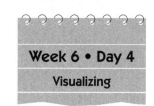

The Lake Cabin

As you read the paragraph, imagine the scene that the words are describing. In the picture below, draw everything that has been left out. Color the picture.

My favorite thing to do in the summer is to go to Grandpa's lake cabin. In the evening after a full day of fishing, Grandpa and I sit on the back porch and enjoy the scenery. The sun setting behind the mountain fills the blue sky with streaks of orange and yellow. Colorful sailboats float by us in slow motion. Suddenly a fish jumps out of the water, making tiny waves in rings. A deer quietly walks to the edge of the water to get a drink. Red and yellow wildflowers grow near the big rock. On the shore across the lake, we see a couple of tents. Someone must be camping there. A flock of geese fly over the lake in the shape of a V. Every time we sit and look at the lake, Grandpa says, "This is the best place on earth!"

On another piece of paper, write a paragraph describing the place that you think is "the best place on earth." Read your paragraph to a friend.

Put the Brakes on Math Mistakes!

Take a look at the signs on Bob's store. Circle any mistakes you see.
Then fix the mistakes so that the signs are correct.

BOB'S BIKE BARN

Bike Helmets $14.999

OPEN 9:30 AM – 8:75 PM

OPEN 8 DAYS A WEEK

* SALE *
$10 off selected Mountain Bikes
Were $139.99
Now $129.00

Handlebar Tape
$3.99 a roll
Buy two for $7.99
SAVE $1.00

Bicycle Baskets
$12.99 each
Two for $25.00
SAVE $.98

* FREE *
Bicycle Stickers
$.10 each

Bicycle Chain
$.50 an inch
That's only $5.00 a foot

½ off all Bicycle seats
Were $17.00
Now $9.50

Where Is Holly?

Drawing conclusions *means to make reasonable conclusions about events in a story using the information given.*

One day, while Mom was washing dishes in the kitchen, she realized that she had not heard a peep out of three-year-old Holly in a long time. The last time she had seen her, she was playing in the living room with some building blocks. "She sure is being good," thought Mom.

Write an *X* next to the best answer.

1. **Why did Mom think Holly was being good?**

   _____ Holly was washing dishes for her.

   _____ Holly was playing with dolls.

   _____ Holly was being so quiet.

After rinsing the last dish, Mom went to the living room to see what Holly had built. But Holly was not there. "Holly! Where are you?" Mom asked. Mom heard a faraway voice say, "Mommy!" So Mom went outside to see if Holly was there.

2. **Why did Mom go outside to look for Holly?**

   _____ Holly's voice sounded so far away.

   _____ The last time Mom saw Holly, she was riding her tricycle.

   _____ Holly said, "I'm outside, Mommy."

Mom looked down the street, up in the tree, and in the backyard, but Holly was not outside. She called her again but did not hear her voice. So, she went back inside. "Holly! Where are you? Come out right now."

3. **Why did Mom say, "Come out right now."**

   _____ She was mean.

   _____ She heard Holly's voice coming from the closet.

   _____ She thought Holly might be hiding.

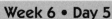
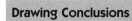

Once again, Mom heard a faraway sound. "Help me!" cried Holly. Mom ran to the bathroom, but Holly was not there. She ran to the garage, but Holly was not there either. Finally, she ran to Holly's room and saw Holly's feet sticking out of the toy box, kicking wildly in the air!

4. **What had happened to Holly?**

_____ **She had fallen headfirst into the toy box and could not get out.**

_____ **She was playing with the blocks again.**

_____ **She was playing hide-and-seek with Mom.**

Mom lifted Holly out of the toy box and asked, "Holly, are you all right?" Holly replied, "I think so." Holly then told Mom that she had been looking for her toy piano because she wanted to play a song for her. "Do you want to hear the song now?" Holly asked. "First, let's have a special snack. You can play the piano for me later," Mom suggested. Holly thought that was a great idea!

5. **Where was Holly's toy piano?**

_____ **The piano was under Holly's bed.**

_____ **The piano was at the bottom of the toy box.**

_____ **She was playing hide-and-seek with Mom.**

Mom and Holly walked to the kitchen. Mom made Holly a bowl of ice cream with chocolate sauce and a cherry on top. Holly told Mom that she wanted to go to the the park. Mom really liked that idea.

6. **What will Mom and Holly do next?**

_____ **Mom and Holly will go shopping.**

_____ **Mom and Holly will go for a bike ride.**

_____ **Mom and Holly will play on the swings in the park.**

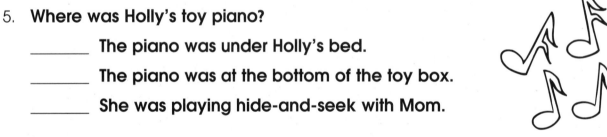

Scholastic Teaching Resources   *Get Ready for 4th Grade*

Helping Your Child Get Ready: Week 7

These are the skills your child will be working on this week.

Math
- reading a table
- word problems
- 2- and 3-digit multiplication
- division
- equivalent fractions

Reading
- reading for details
- identifying story elements

Writing
- sentence elaboration

Vocabulary
- synonyms, antonyms, and homophones

Grammar
- parts of speech

Here are some activities you and your child might enjoy.

Mum's the Word This is a fun dinnertime family game. Agree on a small word that is used frequently in conversation, such as *the* or *and*. This word becomes "mum." No one can say it! Anyone who does, drops out. The last person left is the winner.

Palindrome Collection Palindromes are words that are spelled the same backward and forward. Start a palindrome collection with your child. Here are some to get you going: *bob*, *toot*, *Anna*, and *refer*.

One-Minute Categories Ask your child to name as many examples as possible of a category in one minute. For example, for animal, he or she might name dog, cat, zebra, horse, and so on. Make the categories more challenging as his or her skill increases.

What's the Math Question? Ask your child to make up a question or problem to go with an answer. For example, if you say the answer is "48," he or she could say the question is "What is 12 x 4?" or "What is 54 − 8?"

Your child might enjoy reading the following books.

Little House on the Prairie
by Laura Ingalls Wilder

Liar, Liar, Pants on Fire
by Gordon Korman

Hurricanes: Earth's Mightiest Storms
by Patricia Lauber

_____ 's Incentive Chart: Week 7

Name Here

This week, I plan to read _____ minutes each day.

CHART YOUR PROGRESS HERE.

Week 7	Day 1	Day 2	Day 3	Day 4	Day 5
I read for...	minutes	minutes	minutes	minutes	minutes
Put a sticker to show you completed each day's work.					

Congratulations!

Wow! You did a great job this week!

#1

Place sticker here.

Parent or Caregiver's Signature _____

A Perfect Match?

Each word in column 1 has a match in column 2.
The match in column 2 is either a synonym (means
the same thing, such as *right* and *correct*), antonym
(means the opposite, such as *right* and *wrong*), or
homophone (sounds the same, such as *one* and *won*).
Draw a line between each match and write which type
of match it is. There is only one correct match for each word.

Column 1	Column 2	Type of Match
1. modern	a. where	1. _____
2. sail	b. dusk	2. _____
3. thaw	c. gargantuan	3. _____
4. tired	d. late	4. _____
5. blue	e. sale	5. _____
6. dawn	f. ancient	6. _____
7. right	g. exhausted	7. _____
8. miniscule	h. blew	8. _____
9. wear	j. correct	9. _____
10. tardy	k. freeze	10. _____
11. grate	l. kernel	11. _____
12. assemble	m. live	12. _____
13. danger	n. hazard	13. _____
14. dwell	o. dismantle	14. _____
15. colonel	p. great	15. _____

YOUR TURN

Make a puzzle of your own like the one above. Use synonyms,
antonyms, and homophones. Then have someone in your
family figure out what the matches are.

At the Beach

➡ *A **describing word** makes a sentence more interesting.*

Read the describing words found in the beach balls. Add the describing words to make each sentence more interesting. Write each new sentence.

1. **The snow cone sat in the sun.**

_____

2. **Many children ran toward the ocean waves.**

_____

3. **My friends built a sandcastle.**

_____

4. **My brother grabbed his beach toys.**

_____

5. **Our dog tried to catch beach balls.**

_____

 On another piece of paper, draw a beach ball. Fill it with words that describe a day at the beach.

Scholastic Teaching Resources   *Get Ready for 4th Grade*

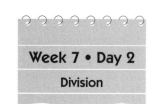

Flying Carpet

Solve the problems. If the answer is between 100 and 250, color the shape red. If the answer is between 251 and 900, color the shape blue. Finish the design by coloring the other shapes with the colors of your choice.

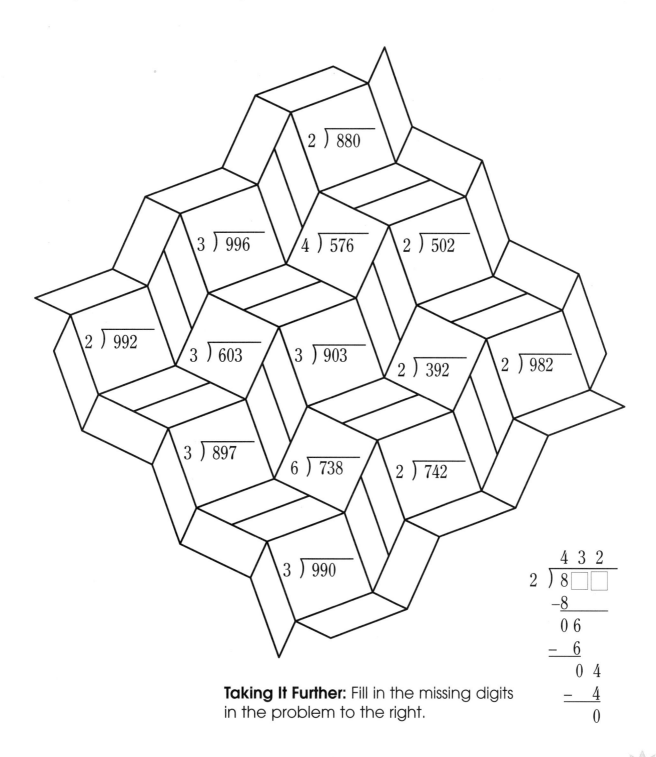

Taking It Further: Fill in the missing digits in the problem to the right.

$$
\begin{array}{r}
4\ 3\ 2 \\
2\ \overline{)\ 8\ \square\ \square} \\
-8 \\
\hline
0\ 6 \\
-\ \ 6 \\
\hline
0\ 4 \\
-\ \ 4 \\
\hline
0
\end{array}
$$

Super Silly Circus

Don't read this story yet! Give it to a member of your family and ask him or her to tell you the parts of speech under the blanks below. You give a word for each part of speech, and your partner writes it in the blank. Then he or she writes the words in the story and reads the story aloud.

1. _____
   YOUR CITY

2. _____
   ADJECTIVE

3. _____
   YOUR LAST NAME

4. _____
   NOUN

5. _____
   ADJECTIVE

6. _____
   VERB + *ER*

7. _____
   ADVERB

8. _____
   VERB

9. _____
   NUMBER

10. _____
    PLURAL NOUN

11. _____
    NOUN

12. _____
    BODY PART

13. _____
    PLURAL NOUN

14. _____
    ADJECTIVE

15. _____
    ADJECTIVE ENDING IN *EST*

Over the summer, the circus came to

_____ . Not just any _____
        1   2

circus, it was the Ringling Brothers and Barnum and

_____ Circus! My favorite performer was
        3

the _____ tamer who was fearless and
              4

_____ . The tightrope _____
        5   6

teetered _____ above the stage, looking
                   7

like she was about to _____ .
                                8

We saw a _____ -foot-tall man juggling
                   9

_____ while wearing a _____
        10   11

on his _____ . All day we ate
                 12

_____ , peanuts, and popcorn
        13

until we felt _____ . It really was
                        14

the _____ show on earth!
              15

Scholastic Teaching Resources   *Get Ready for 4th Grade*

Weatherman

Figure It Out!

1. Showers on Monday morning produced 0.5 inches of rain by noon. By 6 p.m., a total of 2 inches of rain had fallen. How many inches of rain fell between noon and 6 p.m.? _____

2. On Tuesday, 1.2 inches of rain fell. Two more inches of rain fell the next day. How many inches of rain fell on Wednesday? _____

3. The graph shows the high temperatures for Wednesday through Sunday. On which day was the highest temperature reached? The lowest? What was the difference between the two temperatures? _____

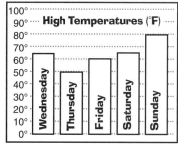

4. Between which two days did the temperature drop 15 degrees? Increase by 15 degrees? _____

5. Saturday's low temperature was 38°. How many degrees did the temperature rise to reach Saturday's high temperature? _____

SUPER CHALLENGE: What was the average high temperature for all five days shown on the graph?

Dining with Dinosaurs

This "Dino" table provides specific information about different kinds of dinosaurs. Use the table to choose the best answer to each question below.

DINOSAUR FACTS				
Name	What It Means	Size	Weight	Food
Ankylosaurus	Crooked lizard	25 feet	3 tons	plants
Baryonyx	Heavy claw	30 feet	3,300 pounds	fish
Eoraptor	Dawn thief	3 feet	11–16 pounds	meat, insects
Maiasaura	Good mother lizard	30 feet	3 tons	plants
Plateosaurus	Broad lizard	20–26 feet	2,000–4,000 lb.	plants
Seismosaurus	Earthquake lizard	120–150 feet	40 tons	plants
Spinosaurus	Spined lizard	40 feet	4 tons	fish
Velociraptor	Fast thief	6 feet	30 pounds	meat

1. How much did the dinosaur called *Maiasaura* weigh?
   a. 30 pounds   c. 4 tons
   b. 3 tons   d. 40 tons

2. Which dinosaur's name means "broad lizard?"
   a. *Ankylosaurus*   c. *Plateosaurus*
   b. *Eoraptor*   d. *Spinosaurus*

3. How many feet long was the dinosaur called *Velociraptor*?
   a. 3 feet   c. 25 feet
   b. 6 feet   d. 30 feet

4. Which of these dinosaurs ate fish?
   a. *Ankylosaurus*   c. *Velociraptor*
   b. *Maiasaura*   d. *Spinosaurus*

5. Which is the largest, heaviest dinosaur listed in the chart?
   a. *Seismosaurus*   c. *Eoraptor*
   b. *Plateosaurus*   d. *Baryonyx*

Wagon Train

Will and Kate thought it would be a great adventure to travel west with the wagon train. In the spring of 1880, their family left their home in Pennsylvania and joined a wagon train headed for California. For months, their only home was the wagon. A large canvas was spread over metal hoops on top of the wagon to make a roof. Will helped his father oil the canvas so that the rain would slide off and keep them dry inside. Each day Kate and Will gathered wood as they walked beside the wagon. In the evening when the wagons stopped, Kate and her mother built a campfire for cooking supper. They hauled supplies with them so that they could cook beans and biscuits. Sometimes the men went hunting and brought back fresh deer meat or a rabbit for stew. When it rained for several days, the roads were so muddy that the wagons got stuck. There was always danger of snakes and bad weather. There were rivers and mountains to cross. There was no doctor to take care of those who got sick or injured. Will and Kate were right. Traveling with a wagon train was a great adventure, but it was a very hard life.

Unscramble the words to make a complete sentence that tells the main idea.

wagon dangerous. on a Life hard and was train _____

_____

Choose a word from the wagon to complete each detail.

1. __ __ __ __ __ __ the canvas

2. __ __ __ __ __ __ __ __ __ wood

3. __ __ __ __ __ __ __ over a campfire

4. __ __ __ __ __ __ __ supplies

5. __ __ __ __ __ __ __ for meat

6. __ __ __ __ __ __ __ __ out for snakes

7. __ __ __ __ __ __ __ for the rain to stop

8. __ __ __ __ __ __ __ __ __ rivers and mountains

9. __ __ __ __ __ __ __ sick or hurt with no doctor to help

getting   gathering   hunting

oiling   waiting   hauling

crossing   cooking   watching

Scholastic Teaching Resources   Get Ready for 4th Grade

Timothy the Tiger

Timothy the tiger is a weight lifter, and he loves to look at himself in the mirror. Only one of the reflections below is his real mirror image. Can you figure out which one it is and circle it? To check your answer, do the multiplication problems below each tiger. The product that matches the number under Timothy is his exact mirror image.

5,618

214
x 36

407
x 22

563
x 17

505
x 18

499
x 12

486
x 13

107
x 34

386
x 24

719
x 12

802
x 11

272
x 19

315
x 22

189
x 41

106
x 53

610
x 11

Why shouldn't you tell secrets to tigers?
Because they carry tails (tales).

Scholastic Teaching Resources Get Ready for 4th Grade

The Math Contest

Story elements *are the different parts of a story. The* **characters** *are the people, animals, or animated objects in the story. The* **setting** *is the place and time in which the story takes place. The* **plot** *of the story includes the events and often includes a* **problem** *and a* **solution***.*

Every Friday, Mr. Jefferson, the math teacher, held a contest for his students. Sometimes they played math baseball. Sometimes they had math relays with flash cards. Other times, they were handed a sheet of paper with a hundred multiplication problems on it. The student who finished fastest with the most correct answers won the contest. One Friday, there was a math bee. It was similar to a spelling bee, except the students worked math problems in their heads. There was fierce competition, until finally, everyone was out of the game except Riley and Rhonda. Mr. Jefferson challenged them with problem after problem, but both students continued to answer correctly every time. It was almost time for class to end, so Mr. Jefferson gave them the same difficult problem. They had to work it in their heads. Riley thought hard and answered, "20." Rhonda answered, "18." Finally they had a winner!

To find out who won the game, work the problem below in your head. Write the answer on the blank.

$$6 + 4 + 6 - 4 - 4 + 6 + 6 = \underline{\hspace{2cm}}$$

Now, to see if you are correct, circle only the 6's and 4's in the box. The answer will appear.

Answer each question below.

7	4	6	5	3	1	2	6	4	8	0
6	9	1	4	3	5	6	2	8	6	7
5	0	8	6	0	4	9	7	3	1	4
3	1	7	4	0	6	5	8	7	2	6
7	0	6	5	8	4	9	3	2	9	6
8	4	9	8	0	6	1	5	7	8	4
6	2	7	3	9	2	4	8	1	6	5
6	4	4	6	1	9	0	6	6	2	3

1. **Name the three people in the story.** _____,
    _____, **and** _____

2. **Circle where the story takes place.**
    a. in the gym   **b. in the cafeteria**   **c. in Mr. Jefferson's classroom**

3. **Circle the problem in the story.**
    a. Mr. Jefferson held the contest on Thursday.
    b. Class was almost over, and the contest was still tied.
    c. Riley and Rhonda both answered incorrectly.

4. **Who answered the difficult question correctly?** _____

It's All the Same!

 Equivalent fractions *have the same amount.*

 $\frac{1}{2} = \frac{4}{8}$ $\frac{3}{6} = \frac{1}{2}$

Write each missing numerator to show equivalent fractions.

A.

$\frac{1}{2} = \frac{}{4}$

B.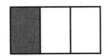

$\frac{1}{3} = \frac{}{6}$

C.

$\frac{1}{4} = \frac{}{8}$

D.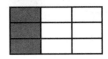

$\frac{1}{3} = \frac{}{9}$

E.

$\frac{1}{5} = \frac{}{10}$

F.

$\frac{1}{2} = \frac{}{8}$

G.

$\frac{1}{2} = \frac{}{16}$

H.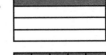

$\frac{1}{4} = \frac{}{20}$

Write the number sentence that shows each set of equivalent fractions.

I.

$\frac{}{} = \frac{}{}$

J.

$\frac{}{} = \frac{}{}$

K.

$\frac{}{} = \frac{}{}$

L.

$\frac{}{} = \frac{}{}$

 Raymond's pizza has been cut into fourths. Debbie's pizza has been cut into eighths. Raymond eats 2/4 of his pizza. Debbie eats 4/8 of her pizza. Did they eat the same amount of pizza? On another piece of paper, draw a picture to show your answer.

Scholastic Teaching Resources *Get Ready for 4th Grade*

Helping Your Child Get Ready: Week 8

These are the skills your child will be working on this week.

Math
- geometry
- word problems

Reading
- finding the main idea

Writing
- using an outline to organize ideas
- expository paragraph

Vocabulary
- portmanteau words
- compound words

Grammar
- punctuation

Handwriting
- writing lowercase cursive letters

Here are some activities you and your child might enjoy.

Word Chain Develop your child's listening skills by playing Word Chain. In this game, someone says a word, and the next person must say a word that begins with the last letter of the previous player's word.

Movie Review Ask your child to write a movie review. Be sure he or she writes the review immediately after the movie—just like real critics do. Encourage him or her to include lots of descriptive words in the review.

Poems to Remember Encourage your child to memorize a short poem. Doing so will require him or her to read a poem over and over—a great way to build reading fluency. You might suggest a poem by Jack Prelutsky or Shel Silverstein. (Their books are readily available at the library.) Give your child plenty of time to learn the poem and then give him or her a chance to recite it to the rest of the family.

Bug Safari Have your child go on a bug safari! Mark off a small section of your backyard or a park. Then start hunting. Have him or her keep a list of the different kinds of creepy crawlies he or she sees. You might want to have a field guide handy so bug identification is easy.

bee

beetle

fly

Your child might enjoy reading the following books.

Pink and Say
by Patricia Polacco

The Adventures of Captain Underpants
by Dav Pilkey

spider

Dear Mr. Henshaw
by Beverly Cleary

ant

grasshopper

ladybug

_____ 's Incentive Chart: Week 8

Name Here

This week, I plan to read _____ minutes each day.

CHART YOUR PROGRESS HERE.

Week 8	Day 1	Day 2	Day 3	Day 4	Day 5
I read for...	minutes	minutes	minutes	minutes	minutes
Put a sticker to show you completed each day's work.					

Congratulations!

Wow! You did a great job this week!

#1

Place sticker here.

Parent or Caregiver's Signature _____

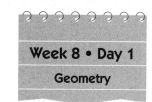

Riddle Teller

Read the riddle. Then draw the shape it describes.

I have 3 sides and 3 corners. One of my corners is at the top.

1.

I have no corners. One half of me is like the other half.

2.

I have 4 corners and 4 sides. You can draw me by joining 2 triangles.

3.

I have 5 sides and 5 corners. Draw a square and a triangle together.

4.

I am not a square, but I have 4 sides and 4 corners.

5.

I have 4 sides and 4 corners. My 2 opposite sides are slanted.

6.

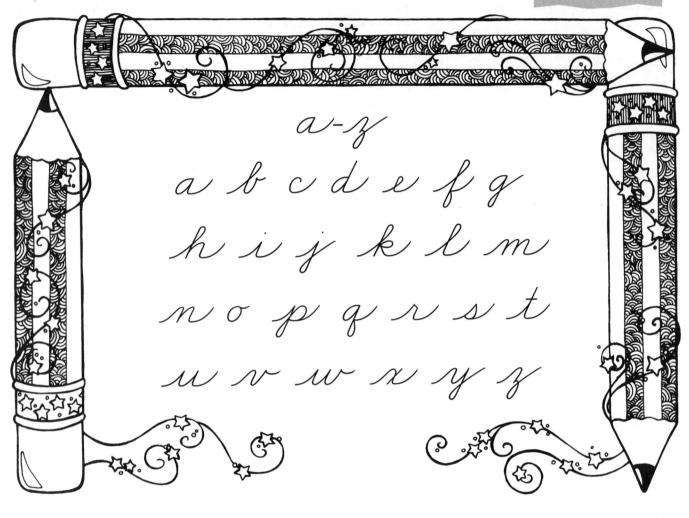

a-z

a b c d e f g

h i j k l m

n o p q r s t

u v w x y z

Write.

_____

_____

_____

_____

_____

Fourteen + Nights = Fortnight

Fortnight *is a word that was formed by blending the sound and meaning of the words* fourteen *and* nights. *It means "two weeks." Here are more words that were formed in a similar way.*

boost	smash	flop	twirl	brunch
motel	smog	telethon	flurry	intercom

What word was made by blending the sound and meaning of each pair of words below? For each pair, choose a word from the box and write it on the line. What does each word mean? Write the letter of the definition for each blended word.

____ 1. **motor + hotel =** _____

____ 2. **breakfast + lunch =** _____

____ 3. **smoke + fog =** _____

____ 4. **twist + whirl =** _____

____ 5. **television + marathon =** _____

____ 6. **flap + drop =** _____

____ 7. **flutter + hurry =** _____

____ 8. **smack + mash =** _____

____ 9. **boom + hoist =** _____

____ 10. **internal + communication =** _____

a. **break violently into pieces**

b. **push from below or behind**

c. **sit or lie down heavily**

d. **a two-way communication system**

e. **late morning meal**

f. **spin rapidly**

g. **a long program for charity**

h. **a form of air pollution**

i. **roadside lodging for travelers**

j. **a sudden outburst**

What Did You Say?

Some stories may include dialogue, or the exact words of story characters. Dialogue lets readers know something about the characters, plot, setting, and problem or conflict in a story. Use quotation marks around a speaker's exact words and commas to set off quotations. Remember to put periods, question marks, exclamation points, and commas inside the quotation marks.

"Get away from my bowl!" yelled Little Miss Muffet when she saw the approaching spider.

"Please don't get so excited," replied the startled spider. "I just wanted a little taste. I've never tried curds and whey before."

Use your imagination to complete the dialogue between the fairy tale or nursery rhyme characters. Include quotation marks and commas where they belong and the correct end punctuation.

1. **When Baby Bear saw the strange girl asleep in his bed, he asked his parents,** _____

   _____

   His mother replied, _____

2. **Humpty Dumpty was sitting on the wall when he suddenly fell off. On the way down**

   he shouted, _____

   Two of the king's men approached. One whispered nervously to the other, _____

   _____

3. **When Jack realized he was about to fall down the hill with a pail of water, he**

   yelled, _____

   _____**cried Jill,**

   as she went tumbling down the hill after Jack.

4. **The wolf knocked on the door of the third little pig's house. When there was no**

   answer, the wolf bellowed, _____

   Knowing that he and his brother were safe inside his sturdy brick house, the third

   little pig replied, _____

   _____

Let's Get Organized

When you write a report or story, it helps to review your notes and organize them into an outline to show the order in which you want to discuss them.

Chester Greenwood → **subject of the report**

I. **Who was Chester Greenwood?** → **main idea becomes topic sentence**
   A. **born in 1858** → **supporting details become supporting sentences**
   B. **grew up in Farmington, Maine**
   C. **as a child had ear problems in winter**

II. **His first invention—earmuffs**
   A. **needed a way to protect ears from cold**
   B. **1873 at age 15 began testing his ideas**
   C. **idea for fur-covered earflaps worked**
   D. **people saw and also wanted earflaps**
   E. **grandmother helped produce them**

III. **His later accomplishments**
   A. **founded a telephone company**
   B. **manufactured steam heaters**
   C. **over 100 inventions**

Study the outline above. Then answer the questions.

1. **What is the topic of the report?** _____

2. **How many paragraphs will there be?** _____

3. **What is main topic of the first paragraph?** _____

   _____

4. **How many details tell about the second main idea?** _____

On another sheet of paper, develop an outline for preparing an interesting and unusual dish that your family enjoys.

White Socks, Black Socks

Figure it out!

1. Rowena Pig is wearing 1 white sock and 1 black sock. What fraction of the socks she's wearing is white? What fraction is black?

_____

2. Rowena puts 7 socks in the washing machine. Four of them are black and 3 are white. What fraction of the socks is black? What fraction is white?

_____

3. Rowena hangs 8 socks out to dry. Two of the socks are black and 6 are white. What fraction is black? Write your answer in simplest form.

_____

4. Judy Frog brings 6 socks on a trip. One third of the socks are red. The rest are green. How many socks are red? How many are green?

_____

5. Six out of 10 socks are blue. The rest are red. What fraction of the socks is red? Write your answer in simplest form.

SUPER CHALLENGE: Judy has 12 socks. One third of them are white. One fourth of them are red. The rest are yellow. How many socks are yellow? How many socks are white and red?

Scholastic Teaching Resources   Get Ready for 4th Grade

Super Duper Lance

 *The **main idea** tells what a story or paragraph is mostly about. **Details** in a story provide the reader with information about the main idea and help the reader better understand the story.*

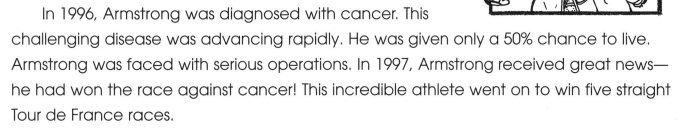

Lance Armstrong is an awesome athlete! This American bicyclist won the Tour de France bicycle race in the summer of 1999. He went on to win it again in 2000, 2001, 2002, and 2003. What makes Armstrong's accomplishment even more amazing is that he was battling cancer before competing in the 1999 Tour de France race.

In 1996, Armstrong was diagnosed with cancer. This challenging disease was advancing rapidly. He was given only a 50% chance to live. Armstrong was faced with serious operations. In 1997, Armstrong received great news— he had won the race against cancer! This incredible athlete went on to win five straight Tour de France races.

The Tour de France is the world's premier cycling event. It takes its competitors all over France, even through the Alps and the Pyrenees Mountains. The course changes each year but is always over 2,000 miles long and always ends in Paris.

Circle the main idea for each paragraph.

1. **Paragraph 1:**

    a. **Armstrong was the first American bicyclist to win the Tour de France.**

    b. **Armstrong is an accomplished bicyclist.**

    c. **Armstrong rides all over France in the summer.**

2. **Paragraph 2:**

    a. **Armstrong was the first American bicyclist to win the Tour de France.**

    b. **Armstrong had cancer in 1996.**

    c. **Armstrong won an important "health" race.**

3. **Paragraph 3:**

    a. **Riders in the Tour de France get to see all of France.**

    b. **Tour de France competitors must be very strong to ride through two mountainous regions.**

    c. **The impressive Tour de France runs all over France and ends in Paris.**

4. Use details from the story to write why you think Armstrong is an accomplished

   athlete. _____

   _____

   _____

   _____

   _____

   _____

5. Write a detail about the Tour de France bicycle race on each tire.

6. What are some of the challenges Armstrong has faced? Which one do you think

   was the most difficult? _____

   _____

   _____

   _____

 Read a magazine article about another sports figure. On another piece of paper, write the main idea of the article.

Scholastic Teaching Resources   *Get Ready for 4th Grade*

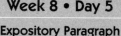

A Paragraph Plan

 Follow these steps in planning a paragraph.
 1. Choose a topic (main idea).
 2. Brainstorm ideas about the topic. (You will need at least three.)
 3. Write a topic sentence.
 4. Write a closing sentence by retelling the topic sentence.

Follow this plan to write a paragraph about Ben Franklin.

1. **Ben Franklin**

2. **a) inventor of bifocal eyeglasses and Franklin stove**
   b) scientist who proved that lightning is electricity
   c) involved in writing the Declaration of Independence

3. **Ben Franklin was a man of many talents.**

4. **Ben Franklin displayed his talents in many ways.**

_____

_____

_____

_____

_____

_____

_____

_____

_____

 Read your paragraph to yourself. Then add a describing word to each supporting sentence.

A Happy Marriage

When you marry or join two different words you create a new word called a "compound word." Look at the list below. Can you figure out the word that can be added to the end of each set of words in these examples to make new compound words? Write the word and the compound words it creates in the blanks. The first one is done for you.

1. half, night, over = *time (halftime, nighttime, overtime)*

2. every, no, some = _____

3. bed, bath, store = _____

4. fire, work, birth = _____

5. soft, kitchen, gift = _____

6. border, bee, on = _____

What word can be added to the *beginning* of each set of words in these examples to make new compound words?

1. ball, line, board = _____

2. proof, color, melon = _____

3. bread, cut, stop = _____

4. ground, pen, mate = _____

5. fish, gaze, struck = _____

6. stairs, side, beat = _____

 **YOUR TURN**

Think of one more set of compound words that use the same word either at the beginning or the end as in the examples above.

Scholastic Teaching Resources   *Get Ready for 4th Grade*

Helping Your Child Get Ready: Week 9

These are the skills your child will be working on this week.

Math
- adding like fractions
- decimals

Reading
- standardized reading test practice
- reading for details

Writing
- topic sentences
- writing a news story

Vocabulary
- content-area vocabulary

Grammar
- possessives

Here are some activities you and your child might enjoy.

Word Box Create a word box by labeling a small box. Invite family members to put interesting words written on slips of paper into the word box. Once a week, take the slips out and talk about the words with your child.

Newspaper Read Aloud Read an article from your newspaper aloud to your child. Choose an article he or she might be interested in to read and discuss.

Family Quiz Show Have your child host your own family quiz show. He or she will need to spend some time writing up questions. The quiz show can be modeled on Jeopardy and include 40 questions that are sorted into categories. Decide on a prize for the winner before you start.

Shopping List Maker Invite your child to become your official shopping list maker. Dictate to him or her all the items you'll need to purchase on your next grocery store visit. This is a great way to building spelling skills

Your child might enjoy reading the following books.

Stage Fright on a Summer Night
by Mary Pope Osborne

William Shakespeare and the Globe
by Aliki

Bunnicula: A Rabbit Tale of Mystery
by Deborah and James Howe

_____'s Incentive Chart: Week 9

This week, I plan to read _____ minutes each day.

CHART YOUR PROGRESS HERE.

Week 9 I read for...	Day 1	Day 2	Day 3	Day 4	Day 5
	minutes	minutes	minutes	minutes	minutes
Put a sticker to show you completed each day's work.					

Congratulations!

Wow! You did a great job this week!

Place sticker here.

Parent or Caregiver's Signature _____

Into Infinity

Solve the problems. Then rename the answers in lowest terms.

If the answer is $\frac{1}{4}$, $\frac{1}{8}$, or $\frac{1}{16}$, color the shape purple.

If the answer is $\frac{1}{2}$, $\frac{1}{3}$, or $\frac{1}{7}$, color the shape blue.

If the answer is $\frac{2}{3}$, $\frac{3}{4}$, or $\frac{7}{8}$, color the shape green.

If the answer is $\frac{3}{5}$, $\frac{4}{5}$, or $\frac{5}{7}$, color the shape yellow.

If the answer is $\frac{9}{10}$ or $\frac{11}{12}$, color the shape red.

Finish the design by coloring the other shapes with colors of your choice.

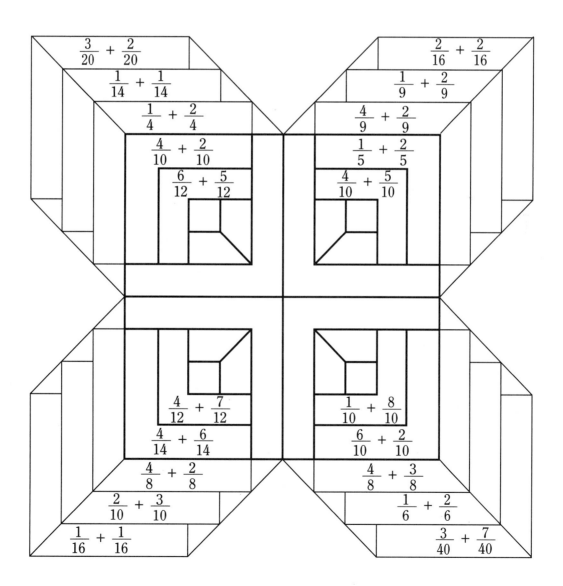

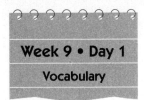

From This to That

Below are three lists of words that have to do with geography, history, and math. You'll need to know the meaning of the words in order to rank them as indicated. If you need help, use a dictionary or other reference source.

1. **Write these geographic terms in order from the** *smallest in area* **to the** *biggest in area***.**

   city   _____

   county   _____

   continent   _____

   town   _____

   hemisphere   _____

2. **Write these historical figures in order from** *earliest time period* **to** *most recent time period***.**

   medieval knight _____

   Pilgrim   _____

   Neanderthal   _____

   Roman gladiator _____

   Viking   _____

3. **Write these number words from** *least in amount* **to** *greatest in amount***.**

   gross   _____

   dozen   _____

   million _____

   billion _____

   score   _____

Scholastic Teaching Resources   *Get Ready for 4th Grade*

Food for Thought

Would you like another serving of potatoes? How much is a serving anyway? For people on diets, it's often hard to determine what a serving is. Luckily, a healthcare company has come up with guidelines that can help people visualize different serving sizes. For example, a medium potato is about the size of a computer mouse. Are you thinking of having a cup of fruit? Think about a baseball—it's about the right size. A cup of chopped vegetables equals a fist. A hockey puck is about the size of an average bagel. For three ounces of meat, visualize a bar of soap, but for three ounces of fish, imagine a checkbook!

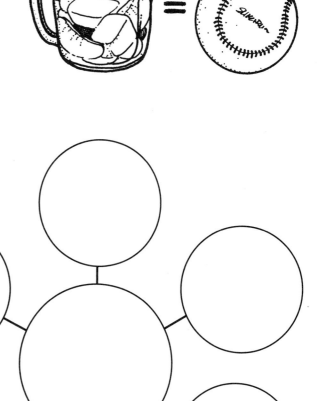

Decide what the main idea of the paragraph is. Write it in the center circle. Find details from the paragraph that tell about the topic. Write them in the web.

 Think of your own visual examples of servings for these foods—1/2 cup of rice, 2 ounces of cheese, and 1 cup of pasta.

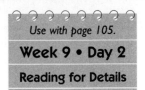
Testing It Out

Use after completing Food for Thought on page 105.
Fill in the circle next to the best answer.

1. The main idea of the passage is that people can use visual guidelines to—
   - (a) make their food taste better
   - (b) figure out the size of a serving of food
   - (c) believe in the success of their diet
   - (d) determine the best way to cook food

2. Visual guidelines for food servings were suggested by a—
   - (a) healthcare company
   - (b) hockey team
   - (c) group of dieters
   - (d) computer company

3. According to the guidelines, a cup of chopped vegetables is about the size of a—
   - (a) baseball
   - (b) hockey puck
   - (c) bagel
   - (d) fist

4. A computer mouse is about the size of—
   - (a) three ounces of fish
   - (b) a medium potato
   - (c) three ounces of meat
   - (d) a cup of fruit

5. You can guess that three ounces of meat—
   - (a) is about what someone on a diet should eat
   - (b) is more than what someone on a diet should eat
   - (c) tastes like a bar of soap
   - (d) tastes better than fish

6. To get the right portions without visual guidelines, you might need a—
   - (a) scale and bar of soap
   - (b) computer mouse and baseball
   - (c) measuring cup and checkbook
   - (d) scale and measuring cup

7. The visual guidelines assume that people know something about—
   - (a) sports and computers
   - (b) exercising to lose weight
   - (c) desserts without sugar
   - (d) healthcare companies

8. These guidelines would be most helpful to people who—
   - (a) learn by doing
   - (b) don't listen well
   - (c) think visually
   - (d) enjoy music

Scholastic Teaching Resources   Get Ready for 4th Grade

What's Wrong With This Picture?

The Halloween Museum may be full of visual treats, but it seems to play tricks on some of the people who work and visit there. It makes them misuse apostrophes. See if you can you find 16 spelling errors that they have made. Write the misspelled words correctly in the appropriate spaces.

Spelling Corrections

Plurals that should end in **-s:**

1. _____
2. _____
3. _____
4. _____
5. _____

Singular possessives that should end in **-'s:**

1. _____
2. _____
3. _____
4. _____
5. _____
6. _____

Plural possessives that should end in **-s':**

1. _____
2. _____
3. _____
4. _____
5. _____

These goblin's are friendly.

These witches broom-sticks are supersonic!

This black cats tail has magical powers'.

Please don't touch the display's or feed the vampire bats!

The werewolves love the full moons light.

Beware! These bats' fangs may scare you!

All the cats eyes look evil!

Those three old lady's fingernails need cleaning!

That werewolf's howl sounds like your fathers voice when he sings.

The werewolves howls give me goosebumps!

Draculas eyes just opened!

The coffins lid has bloodstain's!

Yuk! The cauldron is full of snake's tails and toadstools.

Record-Breaking Trick-or-Treat Bag's

Do not drink from this sorcerers cauldron!

This gentleman's bed is a coffin!

It Just Doesn't Belong!

➡️ *The sentence that tells the topic of a paragraph is called the* **topic sentence**.

Draw a line through the sentence that does not belong with the topic.

Topic: Dogs make great family pets.

Dogs have great hearing, which helps them protect a family from danger.

Most dogs welcome their owners with wagging tails.

My favorite kind of dog is a boxer.

Many dogs are willing to play with children in a safe manner.

Topic: The history of the American flag is quite interesting.

The first American flag had no stars at all.

Not much is known about the history of Chinese flags.

Historians cannot prove that Betsy Ross really made the first American flag.

The American flag has changed 27 times.

Topic: Hurricanes are called by different names depending on where they occur.

Hurricanes have strong, powerful winds.

In the Philippines, hurricanes are called baguios.

Hurricanes are called typhoons in the Far East.

Australian people use the name willy-willies to describe hurricanes.

 Read a paragraph from a favorite chapter book. Read the topic sentence to someone at home.

Scholastic Teaching Resources   *Get Ready for 4th Grade*

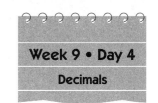

Kaleidoscope of Flowers

If the number has a 5 in the ones place, color the shape green.
If the number has a 5 in the tenths place, color the shape pink.
If the number has a 5 in the hundredths place, color the shape yellow.
Finish the design by coloring the other shapes with colors of your choice.

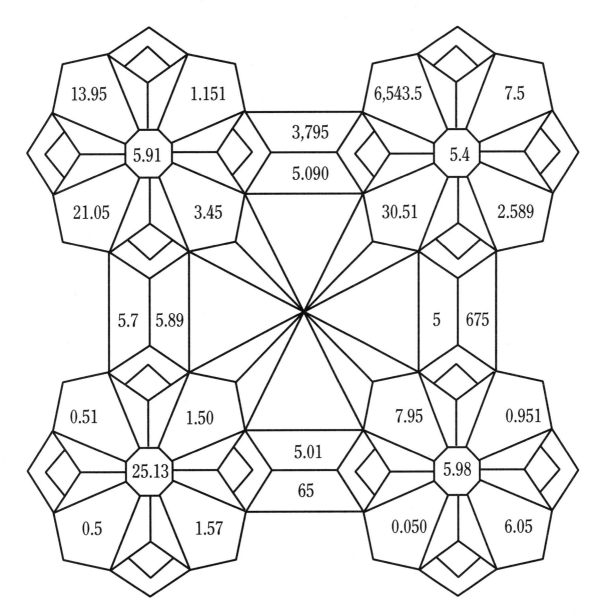

Taking It Further: Place the following decimals in the correct places on the lines below the dots: 4.9, 1.7, 2.5, and 0.2.

Read All About It

A **news story** *reports just the facts about an event and answers the questions* who, what, when, where, why, *and* how. *The most important information is included at the beginning of the article in a paragraph called the* **lead**.

Grass Fires Burn Out of Control   headline

WHERE did it happen? →

GREENSBURG—Grass fires, fueled by wind gusts up to 50 miles per hour, spread into a residential area early Tuesday morning. All residents had to be evacuated. Within minutes over 25 homes were engulfed by flames and destroyed. According to officials, no injuries have been reported.

   Planes and helicopters battling the blaze had to be grounded because the heat of the flames was so intense.

WHY did it happen?

WHEN did it happen?

WHO was affected?

Write a news story using the information below. Remember to write about the facts and events in the order they occurred. Follow the model lead above.

Who: Roseville Emergency Rescue Team
When: April 10, 2003; 5 A.M.
Where: Slate Run River
What: team and rescue vehicles sent;
   worked for three hours; rescued residents
How: used helicopter and boats
Why: residents along river stranded by flash flood after storm

_____

_____ — _____

_____

_____

_____

_____

_____

_____

Use your imagination to write a news story on a piece of paper for one of the following headlines or one of your own.

Mystery of the Missing Dinosaur Solved   **Students Protest School Lunch Menu**

City High Wins Championship   **First Female Elected President**

A Letter from Washington, D.C.

Dear Grandma and Grandpa,

I promised to tell you all about our trip to the nation's capital, but I've been too busy to write! Our stay in Washington, D.C. has been really fun but totally exhausting. We're not going anywhere tonight, so I thought this would be a good time to write.

Today we went to the National Air and Space Museum, my favorite museum so far. Nick liked the Museum of Natural History better. You know how he loves dinosaurs! They have lots of fossils and dinosaur skeletons there. We also saw the Hope Diamond and lots of other beautiful gems. We spent the whole day there yesterday.

Well, I'd better back up and tell you about the things we saw before that. We got here Saturday night and went straight to bed at Aunt Ann's house. The next day we went to the National Zoo. It was raining, so we spent a lot of time looking at reptiles. (They're indoors!) That night we went to a concert with Aunt Ann, but Nick and I didn't like the music very much.

On Monday, we took an elevator to the top of the Washington Monument and got a great view of the city. We studied the map while we were up there so that we would have a better idea of where everything is. Our next stop was the Capitol. We took a tour of the building and saw the House of Representatives and the Senate. In the afternoon, we saw the Lincoln Memorial, the Vietnam Veterans Memorial, and the Jefferson Memorial. You can imagine how tired we were at the end of the day!

On Tuesday, we took a tour of the White House. Then we went to the Museum of American History. Later, we went to the Museum of African Art. Can you believe that just about all the museums here are free? It's so amazing. After supper, we walked in a sculpture garden and then sat on the grass eating ice cream and watching people fly kites. It was a beautiful day.

Tomorrow we're going to visit Mount Vernon in Virginia. That is where George and Martha Washington lived. Then on Saturday we're leaving Washington, D.C. We're going to drive to Assateague Island in Maryland. I'm really excited about seeing the wild ponies there! I'll tell you all about it.

Love,
Alicia

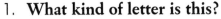

1. **What kind of letter is this?**
   a. a business letter
   b. a thank-you note
   c. an invitation
   d. a friendly letter

2. **Where did Alicia and her family go to get a good view of Washington, D.C.?**
   f. the Washington Monument
   g. the Lincoln Memorial
   h. the Capitol
   j. the Jefferson Memorial

3. **Which museum did Alicia and her family go to first?**
   a. the National Air and Space Museum
   b. the Museum of Natural History
   c. the Museum of American History
   d. the Museum of African Art

4. **Where did Alicia's family go on the day it rained?**

   _____

5. **What did Alicia and her family plan to see in Virginia and Maryland?**

   _____

6. **In the boxes on the left, write two words that describe Alicia. In the boxes on the right, give a detail from the letter to support each word you choose.**

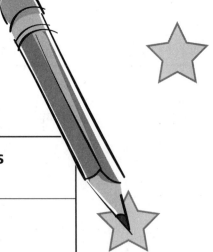

Words That Describe Alicia	Supporting Details

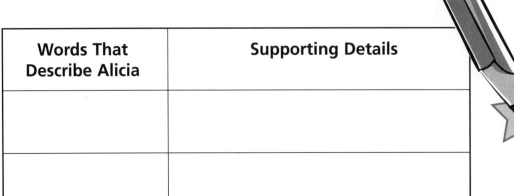

Scholastic Teaching Resources   *Get Ready for 4th Grade*

Helping Your Child Get Ready: Week 10

These are the skills your child will be working on this week.

Math
- area and perimeter
- reading a chart

Reading
- using a graphic organizer to find details
- understanding cause and effect

Writing
- writing a persuasive paragraph
- writing a descriptive paragraph
- proofreading

Vocabulary
- organizing words by their meanings

Grammar
- diagramming sentences
- forming plurals

Here are some activities you and your child might enjoy.

Cartoon Flip Books With a little bit of patience, your child can make his or her own cartoon flip book. Explain that in a cartoon, lots of images—one just slightly different from the last—are put together to make it appear as though a character is moving. For example, here's how to draw a character jumping. Have your child draw a character on the last sheet of a small pad of paper. On the next sheet, have him or her draw the character just a bit above where the character last was. Have your child continue doing this until the entire act of jumping is illustrated. When he or she flips the pages of the book, the character will appear to be jumping.

Constellation Watch Help your child identify a few constellations. Easy ones to start with are the Big Dipper and Orion. Then have him or her research other constellations and their names.

Family Coat of Arms Have your child make a family coat of arms on a piece of posterboard. Have him or her divide a shield shape into quadrants. In each quadrant, he or she can draw a symbol that represents one aspect of your family. Then proudly display your coat of arms.

Sign Your Name Invite your child to learn how to spell his or her name in sign language. He or she can use an encyclopedia or go online to find the sign language alphabet.

C

Your child might enjoy reading the following books.

Seasons: A Book of Poems
by Charlotte Zolotow

First in the Field: Baseball Hero Jackie Robinson
by Derek T. Dingle

James and the Giant Peach
by Roald Dahl

A

B

_____ 's Incentive Chart: Week 10

Name Here

This week, I plan to read_____ minutes each day.

CHART YOUR PROGRESS HERE.

Week 10	Day 1	Day 2	Day 3	Day 4	Day 5
I read for...	minutes	minutes	minutes	minutes	minutes
Put a sticker to show you completed each day's work.					

Congratulations!

Wow! You did a great job this week!

#1

Place sticker here.

Parent or Caregiver's Signature _____

Preview of Prefixes

A prefix is a word part that always comes at the beginning of a word. When a prefix is added to a base word, it changes the word's meaning. The prefix *dis-* means "not." Think about how *dis-* affects the meaning of the words *disloyal, dishonest,* and *disagree.* One meaning for the prefix *re-* is "again." You see this prefix in words such as *redo, rebuild, reconsider,* and *renew.* The meaning of the prefix *over-* is "too much." Some examples of words containing this prefix are *overjoyed, oversleep, overflow,* and *overworked.*

Write the topic and three subtopics on the web. Complete the web by writing details for each subtopic.

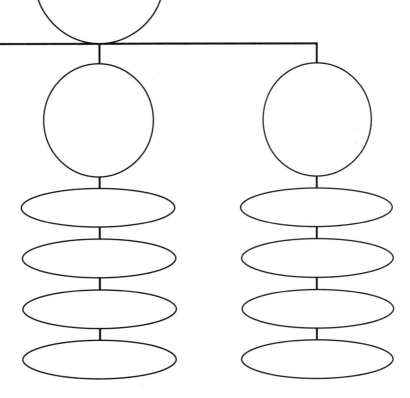

MORE! Find out the meaning of the prefixes *ex-, trans-,* and *inter-.*

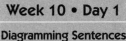

Diagramming Sentences

Diagramming a sentence shows how all the words in the sentence work together.

A. **Underline the articles and adjectives in each sentence. Circle any adverbs. Then diagram each sentence. The model diagram will help you.**

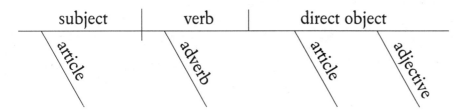

1. The dancer made a graceful movement.

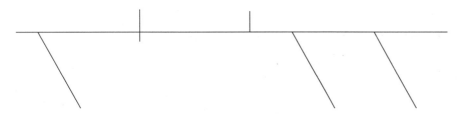

2. The tiny cricket slowly ate the green leaf.

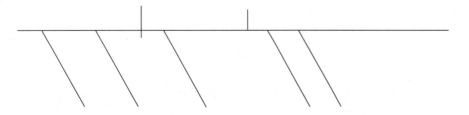

B. **Complete the diagram for the following sentence.**

1. The playful kitten gleefully chased the red ball.

Scholastic Teaching Resources   *Get Ready for 4th Grade*

I'm Sure You'll Agree!

 *A **persuasive paragraph** gives your opinion and tries to convince the reader to agree. Its supporting ideas are reasons that back up your opinion.*

Reason 1

Topic sentence

→ Our family should have a dog for three reasons.

First, pets teach responsibility. If we get a dog, I will

feed him and take him for walks after school. The

second reason for having a pet is that he would ← *Reason 2*

make a good companion for me when everyone else is busy. I won't

Reason 3

drive Dad crazy always asking him to play catch with me. The third ←

reason we need a dog is for safety. He would warn us of danger and

keep our house safe. For all of these reasons, I'm sure you'll agree that

we should jump in the car and head toward the adoption agency right

away. I don't know how we have made it this long without a dog! ← *closing sentence*

Plan and write a persuasive paragraph asking your parents for something (such as a family trip, expensive new shoes, or an in-ground pool).

1. **Choose a topic.** _____

2. **Write a topic sentence.** _____

3. **Brainstorm three supporting reasons.**

   Reason 1 _____

   Reason 2 _____

   Reason 3 _____

 On another piece of paper, use your plan to write a persuasive paragraph.

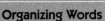

Out of Here!

One item on each list below actually belongs in another list. To get the item "out of here," circle it. Then write the number of the list where it really belongs. When you're done, write what each list is about. The first one is done for you.

List	Circled Word Belongs on List #?	What Is This List About?
1. thigh, (cylinder,) calf	6	parts of a leg
2. slingshot, pavement, tomahawk		
3. pond, palette, lagoon		
4. bog, town, village		
5. jaguar, panther, creek		
6. cube, sphere, triathlon		
7. swamp, marsh, puma		
8. easel, canvas, catapult		
9. blacktop, hamlet, asphalt		
10. decathlon, marathon, shin		

YOUR TURN

Create a chart of your own like the one above but using only four lists. See whether someone in your family can figure out which item doesn't belong, where it should go, and what each list is all about.

Scholastic Teaching Resources   *Get Ready for 4th Grade*

Math's Got It Covered

This soccer player sure has a lot of ground to cover. Just how much exactly? Look at the picture and answer the questions.

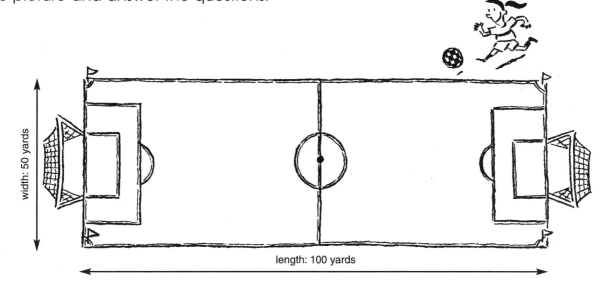

width: 50 yards

length: 100 yards

1. a. **What is the length of the field?**   yards _____   feet _____
   b. **What is the width of the field?**   yards _____   feet _____
   c. **What is the perimeter of the field?**   yards _____   feet _____
   d. **What is the area of the field?**   yards _____   feet _____

2. a. **What is the perimeter of half of the field?**   yards _____   feet _____
   b. **What is the area of half of the field?**   yards _____   feet _____

3. **Imagine a field with a length of 130 yards and a width of 75 yards.**
   a. **What is the perimeter of that field?** _____
   b. **What is the area of that field?** _____

All-Star Math!

Is the perimeter of half the field what you expected? Why or why not?

_____

_____

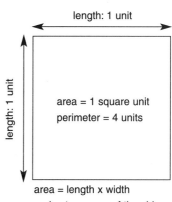

length: 1 unit

length: 1 unit

area = 1 square unit
perimeter = 4 units

area = length x width
perimeter = sum of the sides

Scholastic Teaching Resources   *Get Ready for 4th Grade*

Adorable Animals

Do you know what a baby goat is called? The chart below provides the names for many baby animals. Use the chart to choose the best answer to each question.

NAMES FOR BABY ANIMALS			
Animal	Name for Baby	Animal	Name for Baby
Bear	Cub	Fox	Kit
Cow	Calf	Goat	Kid
Deer	Fawn	Kangaroo	Joey
Dog	Pup	Sheep	Lamb

1. What is the name for a baby deer?
    a. cub   c. fawn
    b. calf   d. pup

2. What is a baby fox called?
    a. kit   c. cub
    b. kid   d. lamb

3. Which kind of animal has cubs?
    a. goat   c. kangaroo
    b. sheep   d. bear

4. A "joey" is what kind of animal?
    a. cow   c. kangaroo
    b. fox   d. sheep

5. A baby goat is a —
    a. kid   c. pup
    b. lamb   d. calf

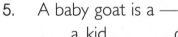

Scholastic Teaching Resources   *Get Ready for 4th Grade*

What's Wrong With This Picture?

Herman Hound is a smart and successful storekeeper, but he sure needs help spelling plurals! Herman knows that you usually add -s to the singular form but that sometimes you must add -es or change the final y of a word to i and then add -es. Help Herman by finding and correcting 16 misspelled plurals in his store.

Magazines and Books

Dog Life

Teen Puppys

Doghouse Beautiful

Canine Digest

Twelve Monthes in the Doghouse

Couchs Are for Sleeping

Mad Dogs and Englishmen

Kittys Beware!

Outfoxing Foxs

A Bird in the Bushes

Warning Signes

Beware the Owner

Skunks Crossing

Danger: Porcupines

Snackes

Trail Mixs

Human Being Crackers

Kitten Kisses

Cat Cookys

Bath Toies

Combs and Brushs

Grooming Department

Powders for Fleas, Ticks, and Flys

Collars and Leashes

Bowls and Dishs

Hunting Supplys

Duck Decoies

Earplugs

Backpacks and Pouchs

Sweaters

A Vivid Picture

 A **descriptive paragraph** creates a vivid image or picture for readers. By choosing just the right adjectives, you can reveal how something looks, sounds, smells, tastes, and feels. Compare the sentences from two different paragraphs. Which one creates a more vivid picture?

The pizza with sausage and onions tasted so good.

The smooth, sweet sauce and bubbly mozzarella topped with bite-sized chunks of extra hot sausage and thin slivers of sweet onion on a perfectly baked, thin crust delighted my taste buds.

Cut out a picture of something interesting and paste it in the box. Then brainstorm a list adjectives and descriptive phrases to tell about it.

Now, write a paragraph about the picture. Begin your paragraph with a topic sentence that will grab readers. Add supporting sentences that include the adjectives and descriptive phrases listed to create a vivid picture.

 Here is a set of adjectives: *bumpy, dusty, narrow, steep, curvy, unpaved, well-worn.* **Think about what they might describe. Then on a piece of paper use the words to write a descriptive paragraph that paints a picture.**

Scholastic Teaching Resources   *Get Ready for 4th Grade*

The Elves of Iceland

If you visited Iceland, would you look for elves? Many people in Iceland believe in elves and other magical folk that can cause mischief. Some Icelanders consult a person called an elf-spotter before building a home. The elf-spotter ensures that the land is elf free. The country's Public Roads Administration has been known to reroute highways because of angry elves. Some Icelandic tourist groups have even made maps charting elf haunts for curious visitors!

Read the cause and one of its effects on the map. Find two other effects in the passage. Write them on the map.

Effects

People consult elf-spotters before building homes.

Cause

Icelanders believe in elves.

→

MORE! Locate Iceland on a globe or world map.

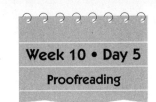

This Day in History

Find and mark the twelve errors. They may be spelling, punctuation, capitalization, or grammar errors.

One Year Ago

National Eat Lunch with a Tree Day was declared a holiday on monday, April 2. No one has figureed out how you would actually eat lunch with a tree. If they do, this will be a great celebration.

37 Years Ago

The excuse, "The dog ate my homwork" was first used by Timmy Murtz of ogden, ohio. Timmy don't actually have a dog—or any homework, for that matter! His techer didn't believe the excuse for even one second.

50 Years Ago

On august 7, the annoying telephone call were invented in Newark, New Jersey. Homeowners were called and ask if they would like a free offer.

100 Years Ago

Scientest Alexander Graham Baloney said that water is actually not wet. It just seems wet because the other things around it are very dry. His idea were later proved to be purely preposterous.

Answer Key

Page 7

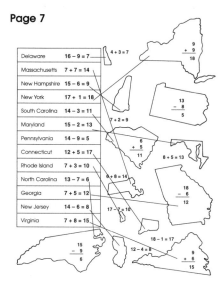

Delaware	16 – 9 = 7
Massachusetts	7 + 7 = 14
New Hampshire	15 – 6 = 9
New York	17 + 1 = 18
South Carolina	14 – 3 = 11
Maryland	15 – 2 = 13
Pennsylvania	14 – 9 = 5
Connecticut	12 + 5 = 17
Rhode Island	7 + 3 = 10
North Carolina	13 – 7 = 6
Georgia	7 + 5 = 12
New Jersey	14 – 6 = 8
Virginia	7 + 8 = 15

Page 8

You're, your, you're, you're, you're, You're, your, you're, You're, your, your, Your, your, You're, your, your, You're, you're, your, Your

Page 9–10

1. Color the picture of Homer in his cage.
2. Homer had many exciting adventures after crawling out of his cage. 3. Answers will vary.

Page 11–12

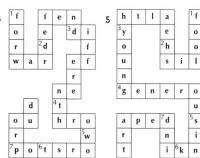

Page 13

324 + 632 = 956; 241 + 551 = 792; 155 + 331 = 486; 213 + 313 = 526; 415 + 322 = 737; 143 + 146 = 289; 202 + 216 = 418; 431 + 422 = 853; 142 + 233 = 375; 541 + 134 = 675; 335 + 333 = 668; 712 + 232 = 944; 220 + 314 = 534; 514 + 334 = 848; 224 + 143 = 367; 416 + 132 = 548; Joe brought $5.40, and Ellie brought $4.35.

Page 14

Answers will vary.

Page 15

1. While I waited for my parents to get home, I watched a movie. 2. My brother was in his room because he had homework to do. 3. Before the movie was over, the power went out. 4. Since this happens all the time, I wasn't concerned. 5. I didn't mind the dark at first until I heard a scratching sound. 6. When I found my flashlight, I started to look around. 7. I was checking the living room when I caught Alex trying to hide.

Page 19

1. pharmacist
2. waiter
3. superintendent
4. merchant
5. astronomer
6. librarian
7. photographer
8. inventor
9. editor
10. dentist

Page 20

1. My sister Annie has always participated in sports, and many say she's a natural athlete. 2. Soccer, basketball, and softball are fun, but she wanted a new challenge. 3. My sister talked to my brother and me, and we were honest with her. 4. I told Annie to go for it, but my brother told her to stick with soccer or basketball. 5. Will Dad convince her to try skiing, or will he suggest ice skating?

Page 21

1. imaginary/make-believe 2. solid/liquid 3. allow/permit 4. terrier/retriever 5. here/hear 6. snake/reptile 7. stroll/walk 8. cord/lamp

Page 22

5,063; 3,721; 3,827; 8,749; ALPS; 8,789; 2,429; 3,012; 5,642; 2,351; ROCKY; 2,429; 5,234; 5,063; 8,789; 5,642; OZARK; 5,063; 6,348; 4,907; 7,483; 8,749; ANDES

Page 23

1. The palindromes are wow, dad, mom, noon, deed. (The other words are not.) 2. screech, pow, slurp, boom, click, sizzle, crunch; 3. knot-not; break-brake; flu-flew; sore-soar; right-write; rode-road; 4. pear, shoe, soccer, like, oven, hen, neither

Page 24

Burgers: O, F; Sports Car: O, F; Inline Skates: O, F; Video Game: F, O; Movie: O, O, F, F, F

Pages 25–26

1. whale shark; 2. pygmy shark; 3. great white shark; 4. mako shark; 5. all; 6. all; 7. goblin shark; 8. hammerhead; 9. all; 10. cookie cutter shark; 11. sawshark; 12. tiger shark

Page 27

A. 15, 18, 21, 24, 27; B. 20, 24, 28, 32, 36; C. 5, 6, 7, 8, 9; D. 28, 35, 42, 49, 56; E. 40, 50, 60, 70, 80; F. 9, 36, 45, 54, 63; G. 18, 24, 36, 42, 48; H. 11, 33, 55, 66; I. 20, 25, 30, 35, 40; J. 16, 32, 48, 56, 64; K. 16, 18, 20, 24, 26; L. 12, 36, 72, 84, 96, 108

Page 28

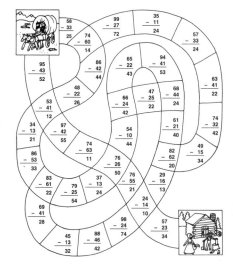

Page 31

4, 6, 1, 3, 5, 2

Page 32

Answers will vary.

Page 33
1. accept
2. dessert
3. angles
4. finale
5. breath
6. loose
7. calendar
8. pasture
9. comma
10. picture

Page 34

Mount Rushmore	Niagara Falls	Gateway Arch	Four Corners Monument	Statue of Liberty
72 − 27 45	57 − 29 28	58 − 39 19	93 − 19 74	94 − 29 65

Grand Canyon	Devil's Tower	Golden Gate Bridge	The Alamo	Old Faithful
82 − 29 53	93 − 14 79	64 − 27 37	66 − 28 38	94 − 28 66

Page 35

Dear Diary,
    Today I get up. I did some scrathing because my neck itched. Then I slept. Then I did some sniffing around. Then I slept. Then I barked at the mailman. After that, I took a nap until dinnertime. for dinner, I had pellets in a dish. then I went back to sleep.
Yours truly, Louie

Dear Diary,
    Today I saw a small white cat out in the yard. This really made me mad! So I barked a lot. I felt better afterwards. Do you know what I ate for dinner? I ate pellets! I washed it all down with a big slurp of water. Then I went back to sleep.
Yours truly, Louie

Dear Diary,
    I just felt like barking today. So I barked and barked. Then I ate pellets and went to sleep.
Yours truly, Louie

Dear Diary,
    That mailman comes every day. I'm getting tired of barking at him. But I did it anyway! Also, I took a walk. Tomorrow I'll catch up on my sleeping.
Yours truly, Louie

Page 36
S. $91.83, L. $70.55, R. $12.73, E. $41.96, S. $34.15, S. $64.30, T. $24.88, Y. $71.40, N. $50.25, S. $37.99, U. $32.76, G. $13.45, A. $90.42, ULYSSES S. GRANT

Pages 37–38
1. B, 2. E, A, D, 3. G, 4. F, 5. C, F

Page 39
Adjectives will vary.

Page 40
1. pop; 2. phon; 3. pos; 4. port; 5. photo
Answers will vary.

Page 43
A. 100; B. 42; C. 30; E. 49; F. 27; G. 3; H. 81; I. 72; L. 24; M. 18; N. 96; O. 36; P. 132; Q. 64; R. 20; S. 54; T. 0; U. 40; V. 21; Y. 16; Every problem they encounter in life becomes a challenge to conquer!

Page 44
Answers and sentences will vary.

Page 45
1–5: Child should note that in each analogy, the first item in the word pair is a part of the second item.

Page 46
E. 9 R3; L. 9 R2; S. 9 R4; O. 4 R4; T. 3 R5; N. 7 R5; P. 6 R3; I. 7 R3; O. 4 R3; A. 8 R6; T. 8 R2; S. 6 R1; H. 5 R3;! 6 R3; R. 5 R2; N. 9 R7; NO, ON THE STAIRS!

Pages 47–48
1. way back yonder—many years ago; 2. buckboard—wagon; 3. Lend me your ears.—Listen to me.; 4. Put a spring in your step—makes you feel peppy; 5. heavenly elixir—wonderful tonic; 6. special blend of secret ingredients—I won't tell what's in it; 7. bustin' broncs—making wild horses gentle; 8. war whoop—loud yell; 9. It's a steal!—You are getting it for a low price.; 10. mosey—walk slowly; 11. kept my eye on him—watched him closely; 12. hornswoggled—cheated; tricked; 13. hightailed it—ran quickly; 14. no-good varmint—evil creature; 15. behind bars—in jail

Page 49
1. in a cave; 2. at a movie; 3. on a roller coaster; 4. on an airplane; 5. at a wedding; 6. at the vet; 7. at a candy store; 8. in a garden

Page 50
A. 1. Mrs. Wu's bank is located at 92 Maple Avenue, Inwood, Texas 75209.
2. September 8, 2001
3. Lakewood, Texas
4. weekdays, Saturdays, and some evenings
5. Saturdays, Sundays, and all holidays
6. Ms. Ames, Mr. Pacheco, and Mrs. Jefferson
7. checks, bills, and deposits
8. May 2, 1974
B. 1. "My favorite author is Jerry Spinelli," said Rick.
2. Spinelli was born on February 1, 1941.
3. His hometown is Norristown, Pennsylvania.
4. "What are your favorite books by him?" asked Theresa.
5. "I like Maniac Magee, Dump Days, and Fourth Grade Rats," replied Rick.

Page 51
Overused words in paragraph:
good, nice, little, big, bad, hard, afraid, sad;
Synonyms will vary.

Page 52
A. 1/4, 2/4,1/2, 3/8, 1/3;
B. 5/6, 4/8, 4/8, 4/10, 5/9;
C. 1/5, 2/4, 2/6, 4/12, 6/12

Page 55
Responses will vary.

Page 56
1. a. went to bed
2. a. worthless
3. c. sad
4. b. not to my liking
5. a. agree
6. b. stirs a memory
7. c. joyous
8. b. having a friendly chat
9. a. give up
10. b. kept from laughing

Page 57
The correct path goes through: 1. shouldn't (Slow Town) 2. isn't (Beachville) 3. We're (Hillville) 4. couldn't (Plains City) 5. there's (State Park) 6. let's (Twin City) 7. we've (Ocean Beach)

Page 58
Main idea: Elephants have very useful noses.;
Sentences that do not belong: Some people like to ride on elephants. Giraffes are the tallest animals in the world.
(The rest of the sentences are details.)

Page 59
Sentences will vary.

Page 60

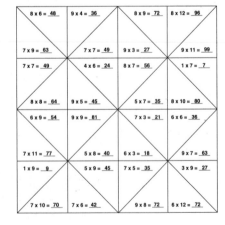

8 × 6 = 48	9 × 4 = 36	8 × 9 = 72	8 × 12 = 96
7 × 9 = 63	7 × 7 = 49	9 × 3 = 27	9 × 11 = 99
7 × 7 = 49	4 × 6 = 24	8 × 7 = 56	1 × 7 = 7
8 × 8 = 64	9 × 5 = 45	5 × 7 = 35	8 × 10 = 80
6 × 9 = 54	9 × 9 = 81	7 × 3 = 21	6 × 6 = 36
7 × 11 = 77	5 × 8 = 40	6 × 3 = 18	9 × 7 = 63
1 × 9 = 9	5 × 9 = 45	7 × 5 = 35	3 × 9 = 27
7 × 10 = 70	7 × 6 = 42	9 × 8 = 72	6 × 12 = 72

Page 61
1. chicken nuggets; 2. green beans; 3. applesauce; 4. roll; 5. carrots; 6. corn; 7. salad

Scholastic Teaching Resources   Get Ready for 4th Grade

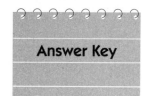

Answer Key

Page 62
A. 1. past
2. past
3. present
4. past
5. past
6. past
7. present
8. present
9. present
10. past

B. 1. The man <u>crossed</u> the river.
2. He <u>rows</u> his boat.

Page 63
57 x 73 = 4161; 98 x 34 = 3332; 23 x 13 = 299;
30 x 42 = 1260; 21 x 61 = 1281; 44 x 20 = 880;
87 x 33 = 2871; 79 x 12 = 948; 81 x 14 = 1134;
55 x 13 = 715; 58 x 42 = 2436; 25 x 13 = 325;
60 x 33 = 1980; 61 x 11 = 671; 72 x 32 = 2304;
41 x 23 = 943; 16 x 34 = 544; 53 x 73 = 3869;
27 x 34 = 918; 71 x 17 = 1207; 49 x 52 = 2548;
83 x 17 = 1411; 25 x 46 = 1150; 95 x 36 = 3420;
25 x 17 = 425; 62 x 12 = 744; 23 x 45 = 1035;
26 x 35 = 910; 37 x 11 = 407; 24 x 20 = 480

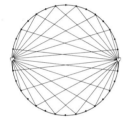

Page 64
1st Alicia
2nd Emily
3rd Asher
4th Grace
5th Dillon
6th Finn

Page 67
Dear Cinderella and Prince Charming,
There must be a terrible mistake! The stepsisters and I have not yet received an invitation to your wedding. I keep telling the stepsisters that the invitation will arrive soon. I'm getting worried that our invitation got lost. I hear you often have problems with the unicorns that deliver the palace mail.
I'm sure you intend to invite us! After all, you were always my special favorite. How I spoiled you! I let you do all the best chores around the house. Are you still mad about that trip to Disney World? I don't know how we could have forgotten you! Anyway, Florida is too hot in the summer.
So, Cinderella, dear, please send along another invitation as soon as you can. I know how busy you are in your new palace. If you need any cleaning help, I can send one of your stepsisters along. They both miss you so much!
Best wishes,
Your not really so wicked stepmother

Page 68
1. 4; 2. 2; 3. 6; 4. 5; 5. 8; 6. 3 remainder 2;
7. 6 remainder 6; 8. 9 remainder 2;
9. 8 remainder 1; 10. 15 remainder 2;
What kind of tools do you use for math?
"Multi"pliers

Page 69
Across	Down
1. tasteless	1. timid
4. calm	2. safe
5. few	3. stingy
6. rude	7. unknown
10. tiny	8. silly
11. careless	9. unclear

Page 70
A. 1. Can we take a taxi downtown?
2. Where does the bus go?
3. The people on the bus waved to us.
4. We got on the elevator.
5. Should I push the elevator button?
B. Answers will vary.

Page 71
Sentences will vary.

Page 72
1. We are eating out tonight because Mom worked late. 2. We are going to Joe's Fish Shack although I don't like fish. 3. Dad said I can play outside until it's time to leave. 4. We can play video games while we are waiting for our food. 5. We may stop by Ida's Ice Cream Shop after we leave the restaurant.

Page 73
Check child's drawings.

Page 74
Accept reasonable corrections. Mistakes: 8 days a week should be 7; 8:75 p.m. is not possible; $10.99 off mountain bikes; bicycle chain is $6.00 a foot; bike helmets are $14.99; you save only $.01, not $1.00, on 2 rolls of tape; free stickers can't be 10 cents each; half-price bicycle seats should be $8.50. The additional mistake: a clock with three hands.

Page 75–76
1. Holly was being so quiet. 2. Holly's voice sounded so far away. 3. She thought Holly might be hiding. 4. She had fallen headfirst into the toy box and couldn't get out. 5. The piano was at the bottom of the toy box. 6. Mom and Holly will play on the swings in the park.

Page 79
1. f. modern/ancient (antonym) 2. e. sail/sale (homonym) 3. k. thaw/freeze (antonym)
4. g. tired/exhausted (synonym) 5. h. blue/blew (homonym) 6. b. dawn/sunset (antonym)
7. j. right/correct (synonym)
8. c. miniscule/gargantuan (antonym)
9. a. wear/where (homonym) 10. d. tardy/late (synonym) 11. p. grate/great (homonym)
12. o. offer/refuse (antonym)
13. n. danger/hazard (synonym)
14. m. dwell/live (synonym) 15. l. colonel/kernel (homonym)

Page 80
Possible answers: 1. The melting snow cone sat in the bright sun. 2. Many excited children ran toward the crashing ocean waves. 3. My new friends built a large sandcastle. 4. My younger brother grabbed his favorite beach toys.
5. Our playful dog tried to catch flying beach balls.

Page 81
880 ÷ 2 = 440; 996 ÷ 3 = 332; 576 ÷ 4 = 144;
502 ÷ 2 = 251; 992 ÷ 2 = 496; 603 ÷ 3 = 201;
903 ÷ 3 = 301; 392 ÷ 2 = 196; 982 ÷ 2 = 491;
897 ÷ 3 = 299; 738 ÷ 6 = 123; 742 ÷ 2 = 371;
990 ÷ 3 = 330

```
        4 3 2
   2 ) 8 6 4
     - 8
       0 6
       - 6
         0 4
         - 4
           0
```

Page 82
Answers will vary.

Page 83
1. 1.5 inches
2. 3.2 inches
3. highest: Sunday; lowest: Thursday; 30 degrees
4. between Wednesday and Thursday;
between Thursday and Saturday
5. 27 degrees
Challenge: 64 degrees

Page 84
1. b. 3 tons
2. c. Plateosaurus
3. b. 6 feet
4. d. Spinosaurus
5. a. Seismosaurus

Page 85
Life on a wagon train was hard and dangerous.; 1. oiling; 2. gathering; 3. cooking;
4. hauling; 5. hunting; 6. watching; 7. waiting;
8. crossing; 9. getting

Page 86
Row 1—7,704; 8,954; 9,571; 9,090; 5,988
Row 2—6,318; 3,638; 9,264; 8,628; 8,822
Row 3—5,168; 6,930; 7,749; 5,618 (circle number), 6,710

Page 87
The answer is 20.
1. Mr. Jefferson, Riley, Rhonda; 2. C; 3. B; 4. Riley

Page 88
A. 2; B. 2; C. 2; D. 3; E. 2; F. 4; G. 8; H. 5;
I. 1/2 = 6/12; J. 1/3 = 2/6; K. 1/6 = 3/18;
L. 1/2 = 3/6

Page 91
Check child's drawings.

Scholastic Teaching Resources   Get Ready for 4th Grade

Page 93

1. i motel
2. e brunch
3. h smog
4. f twirl
5. g telethon
6. c flop
7. j flurry
8. a smash
9. b boost
10. d intercom

Page 94

Sentences will vary.

Page 95

Paragraphs and paragraph plans will vary.

Page 96

1. 1/2 2. 4/7; 3/7 3. 1/4; 3/4; 4. red–2; green–4;
5. 2/5 Challenge: 4–white; 3–red; 5–yellow

Page 97–98

1. b; 2. c; 3. c; 4. Answers will vary. 5. Answers will vary. Sample answers: The course for the Tour de France changes each year. The course is always over 2,000 miles long. 6. Armstrong faced the challenges of battling cancer and competing in the Tour de France.
Opinions will vary.

Page 99

Paragraphs will vary.

Page 100

Word that can be attached to the end:
2. thing (everything, nothing, something)
3. room (bedroom, bathroom, storeroom)
4. place (fireplace, workplace, birthplace)
5. ware (software, kitchenware, giftware)
6. line (borderline, beeline, online)
Word that can be attached to the beginning:
1. base (baseball, baseline, baseboard)
2. water (waterproof, watercolor, watermelon)
3. short (shortbread, shortcut, shortstop)
4. play (playground, playpen, playmate)
5. star (starfish, stargaze, starstruck)
6. up or down (upstairs/downstairs, upside/downside, upbeat/downbeat)

Page 103

3/20 + 2/20 = 1/4; 2/16 + 2/16 = 1/4;
1/14 + 1/14 = 1/7; 1/9 + 2/9 = 1/3;
1/4 + 2/4 = 3/4; 4/ 9 + 2/9 = 2/3
4/10 + 2/10 = 3/5; 1/5 + 2/5 = 3/5;
6/12 + 5/12 = 11/12; 4/10 + 5/10 = 9/10;
4/12 + 7/12 = 11/12; 1/10 + 8/10 = 9/10
4/14 + 6/14 = 5/7; 6/10 + 2/10 = 4/5;
2/10 + 3/10 = 1/2; 1/6 + 2/6 = 1/2
1/16 + 1/16 = 1/8; 3/40 + 7/40 = 1/4

Page 104

1. town, city, county, continent, hemisphere
2. Neanderthal, Roman Gladiator, Viking, medieval knight, Pilgrim
3. dozen, score, gross, million, billion

Page 105

Topic: Visual Guidelines for Food Servings;
Details: medium potato = computer mouse;
cup of chopped vegetables = fist; average bagel = hockey puck; 3 ounces of meat = bar of soap; 3 ounces of fish = checkbook

Page 106

1. B 2. A 3. D 4. B 5. A 6. D 7. A 8. C

Page 107

Plurals that should end in –s: goblins, Bags, powers, stains, displays
Singular possessives that should end in –'s: Cat's, sorcerer's, moon's, coffin's, Dracula's, father's
Plural possessives that should end in –s': witches', ladies', cats', werewolves', snakes'

Page 108

Sentences that do not belong: My favorite kind of dog is a boxer.; Not much is known about the history of Chinese flags.; Hurricanes have strong, powerful winds.

Page 109

Page 110

Responses will vary.

Page 111–112

1. D; 2. F; 3. C; 4. The National Zoo; 5. They were going to see Mount Vernon in Virginia and the wild ponies in Maryland.; 6. Examples: Alicia is enthusiastic (or excited). She raves about how exciting everything is. She is honest. She admits that she did not like the music at the concert. She is appreciative. She enjoys the beautiful days, and she likes that the museums are free.

Page 115

Prefixes; dis- (not): disloyal, dishonest, disagree; re- (again): redo, rebuild, reconsider, renew; over- (too much): overjoyed, oversleep, overflow, overworked

Page 116

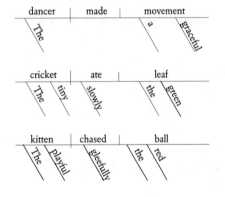

Page 117

Paragraph plans and paragraphs will vary.

Page 118

2. pavement (9 / weapons) 3. palette (8 / bodies of water) 4. bog (7 / communities) 5. creek (3 / big cats) 6. triathlon (10 / three-dimensional objects) 7. puma (5 / wet areas of land) 8. catapult (2 / painting terms) 9. hamlet (4 / road surfaces) 10. shin (1 / track and field events)

Page 119

1a. 100 yards, 300 feet
1b. 50 yards, 150 feet
1c. 300 yards; 900 feet
1d 5,000 square yards, 45,000 square feet
2a. 200 yards, 600 feet
2b. 2,500 square yards, 22,500 square feet
3a. 410 yards
3b. 9,750 square yards
All-Star Math: Answers will vary.

Page 120

1. c; 2. a; 3. d ; 4. c; 5. a

Page 121

Words that end in –s: signs, snacks, toys, months, decoys
Words that end in –es: brushes, mixes, pouches, couches, foxes, dishes
Words that end in –ies: flies, cookies, supplies, puppies, kitties

Page 122

Paragraphs will vary.

Page 123

Effects: Public Roads Administration reroutes highways; tourist maps show elf haunts.

Page 124

One Year Ago
National Eat Lunch with a Tree Day was declared a
(cap) holiday on monday, April 2. No one has figured out how you would actually eat lunch with a tree. If they do, this will be a great celebration.

37 Years Ago
The excuse, "The dog ate my homework" was first used by
(cap) Timmy Murtz of ogden, ohio. Timmy ~~don't~~ didn't actually have (cap) a dog—or any homework, for that matter! His teacher didn't believe the excuse for even one second.

50 Years Ago
(cap) On august 7, the annoying telephone call ~~were~~ was invented in Newark, New Jersey. Homeowners were called and ~~ask~~ asked if they would like a free offer.

100 Years Ago
Scientest Alexander Graham Baloney said that water is actually not wet. It just seems wet because the other things around it are very dry. His idea ~~were~~ was later proved to be purely preposterous.